DEFOE IN SCO.

First published in 2006

Scottish Cultural Press
Unit 6, Newbattle Abbey Business Park
Newbattle Road, Dalkeith EH22 3LJ Scotland
Tel: +44 (0)131 660 6366 • Fax: +44 (0)870 285 4846
Email: info@scottishbooks.com
website: **www.scottishbooks.com**

British Library Cataloguing in Publication Data
A catalogue record for this book is available from the British Library

ISBN-10: 1 84017 052 2
ISBN-13: 978 1 84017 052 8

Printed and bound by Biddles Ltd, King's Lynn, Norfolk

Defoe

in

Scotland

A Spy Among Us

Anne McKim

SCOTTISH CULTURAL PRESS
www.scottishbooks.com

Daniel Defoe, Jure divino (1706),
Alexander Turnbull Library,
Wellington, New Zealand
(SPC-03-596)

Contents

ACKNOWLEDGEMENTS

I am grateful to the Faculty of Arts and Social Sciences at the University of Waikato for research grants to produce this book.

My thanks are also due to the librarians and curators of various special collections in New Zealand and Scotland who assisted me in many ways, and particularly to the staff in the Reference Section of Waikato University Library who expedited my many interloan requests.

I would also like to acknowledge the wonderful research assistance provided by Catherine Stevens and Helen O'Carroll, and the enthusiasm and forebearance of the graduate students in my Honours classes of 2003 and 2004 who heard a great deal more about Defoe than they were led to expect from the course description.

Dramatis Personae

Anne (1665–1714), daughter of James VII and II, and the last ruling Stuart monarch.

Argyll, John Campbell, second Duke of Argyll and Duke of Greenwich (1680–1743). Appointed Lord High Commissioner in 1705; leading advocate of the Union. As Commander-in-Chief of George I's army in Scotland, he led the government troops against **Mar**'s Jacobite army at Sheriffmuir in 1715.

Atholl, John Murray, first Duke of Atholl (1660–1724), and a leading opponent of the Union. A Jacobite sympathiser at the time of the 1708 rising, he was a Hanoverian supporter during the 1715 rebellion, although three of his sons were followers of the old **Pretender**. Famous for his capture of **Rob Roy** in 1717.

Belhaven, John Hamilton, second Lord Belhaven (1656–1708). Member of the Scottish Parliament and a director of the Scottish Trading Company responsible for the Darien expedition. He was a fervent anti-Unionist and made a famous, impassioned speech against it, which Defoe satirised in his poem 'The Vision' (1706). He was arrested on suspicion of supporting a projected French invasion in 1708, and died in London in June that same year. Defoe visited him in prison and later wrote an obituary, which appeared in his *Review*.

Byng, Admiral George, Viscount Byng of Torrington (1663–1733). Led naval forces that thwarted Jacobite invasions from the continent in 1708 and 1715.

Breadalbane, John Campbell, first Earl of Breadalbane and Holland (1634–1717). A Jacobite sympathiser and patron of **Rob Roy** MacGregor. He sent two of his regiments to assist **Mar** in the 1715 rising.

Camden, William (1551–1623). Historian whose *Britannia*, a chorographical description of Britain and Ireland, was very influential.

Cameron, Richard (1648–1680), a Covenanter and field preacher. His followers, known as Cameronians, rejected the Revolution Settlement (1689–1690) which established the Church of Scotland.

Coul, Sir John MacKenzie, third Baronet of Coul (*d*.1728). Chief of the MacKenzie clan, second only to the Campbells in size, and loyal to the Stuarts.

Chevalier de St George, see under **Pretender**.

Clerk, Sir John Clerk of Penicuik, second Baronet (1676–1755). Scottish MP, Treaty Commissioner, and member of **Queensberry**'s circle. Defoe seems to have first met him in London.

Dalrymple, Sir David, of Hailes (*c*.1665–1721). Lord Advocate and Solicitor-General of Scotland. Younger brother of Sir Hew Dalrymple (below).

Dalrymple, Hew, first Baronet, Lord North Berwick (1652–1737). Lord President of the Scottish Court of Sessions and pro-Unionist.

Dundee, John Graham of Claverhouse, Viscount Dundee (1648–89). Army officer and sheriff who ruthlessly suppressed the Cameronians in the south-west of Scotland, he was loyal to James VII and died leading the Jacobite troops to victory at Killiecrankie in July 1689.

Finlay. Defoe identifies him as an old soldier of the Dumbarton regiment and a Jacobite leader in his letters to Harley, but he is otherwise unknown.

Fletcher of Saltoun, Andrew Fletcher of Saltoun (1653–1716). MP for Haddingtonshire and leading figure in the opposition Country Party. Opposed an incorporating union with England, favouring an autonomous Scottish Parliament within a federal alliance.

Godolphin, Sidney, first Earl of Godolphin (1645–1712). Lord Treasurer under both **William III** and Queen **Anne** (1699–1710). Responsible for the successful introduction of the Act of Union.

Hamilton, James Douglas, fourth Duke of Hamilton (1658–1712). Leader of the Country Party, Jacobite sympathiser and vehement opponent of the Union. In the July 1703 session of the Scottish Parliament he confounded his own party by supporting the vote that the nomination of commissioners to treat for a Union with England should be left to Queen **Anne**. He voted against almost every article of the Union treaty. Chosen as one of the sixteen Scottish representative peers to sit in the united British Parliament in 1710.

Harley, Robert, first Earl of Oxford and Mortimer (1661–1724). Speaker of the House of Commons from 1701, he became Secretary of State for the north in 1704 and secured Defoe's services that same year. He became leader of a coalition of Whigs and moderate Tories, and from 1710 Chancellor of the Exchequer and head of a Tory ministry.

Haversham, Lord John Thompson, first Baron Haversham (1648–1710). A vocal English opponent of an incorporating union, he attacked Defoe in print on a number of occasions.

Hepburn, John (1649–1723). Covenanting preacher. Anti-Unionist and anti-Jacobite, he raised his supporters, the Hebronites, in arms against the rebels in 1715.

Macmillan, John (1669–1753). Presbyterian minister at Balmaghie, Kirkcudbrightshire, who became a leader of the Cameronian Covenanters.

Macneil, John. Probationer and preacher who assisted John Macmillan.

Mar, John Erskine, sixth Earl of Mar (1675–1732). A pro-Unionist, he was appointed Secretary of State for Scotland in 1705 and one of the commissioners who drafted and negotiated the Treaty of Union. Disaffected after the accession of George I, he rallied the Jacobites at Braemar in July–August 1715, but retired to France after the inconclusive battle of Sheriffmuir in November 1715.

Montrose, James Graham, fourth Marquis of Montrose and first Duke of Montrose (1682–1742). Member of the Equivalents Committee, which sought Defoe's advice on customs and excise duties. He seems to have befriended Defoe.

Nottingham, Daniel Finch, 2nd Earl of Nottingham, 7th Earl of Winchilsea (1647–1730), statesman. Under **William** and Mary, he was Secretary of State for the North, including Scotland, from 1689–93.

Paterson, William (1658–1719). Born in Dumfriesshire, Scotland and raised in England, be became the founder of the Bank of England (1694) and one of the projectors of the Darien Scheme. Supported the Treaty of Union, and was employed by **Harley** to promote it in Scotland. He drafted a number of the treaty articles relating to trade.

Pierce, John (c.1673–c.1740). Defoe's agent in the west of Scotland. Known to have fled to Scotland in 1705 to evade arrest on seditious libel charges.

Pitcairn, Archibald (1652–1713), natural historian and physician.

Pretender, James Francis Stuart (1688–1766), the 'Old Pretender'. Son of James VII and II, claimant to the thrones of England, Scotland and Ireland, and father of Charles Edward Stuart, the 'Young Pretender', aka Bonnie Prince Charlie. Several Jacobite rebellions, notably in 1708, 1715 and 1719, aimed at placing him on the throne.

Queensberry, James Douglas, second Duke of Queensberry (1662–1711). Reputedly, the first Scot to declare allegiance to **William of Orange**. He fought against **Dundee** and the Jacobite rebels in 1689. First appointed High Commissioner 1699–1702, then again by **Anne** (who also made him a Secretary of State for Scotland), and then Lord Treasurer in 1705. He played a vital role in the negotiation and ratification of the Union articles, for which he was rewarded with a British peerage, becoming the first Duke of Dover (1708). Defoe dedicated his poem *Caledonia* (1706) and his *History of the Union* (1709) to him.

Radcliffe, John (*c.*1650–1714), physician to the courts of James II and then William III.

Rob Roy MacGregor, or Robert Campbell (1671–1734). Cattle dealer, cattle raider. Fought as a Stuart supporter under Viscount **Dundee** at Killiecrankie and led the MacGregors during the Jacobite rising of 1715, but his role at the Battle of Sheriffmuir is disputed by historians. A recent study accuses him of being a Hanoverian spy. He was captured by the Duke of **Atholl** in 1717, but escaped.

Sibbald, Sir Robert (1641–1722), an eminent Edinburgh physician, geographer and natural historian.

Tweeddale, John Hay, second Marquis of Tweeddale (1645–1713). Member of the opposition Country Party, he became a leader of the breakaway New Party, or *Squadrone Volante*, a political group whose votes ensured the passage of the Act of Union in Scotland.

William, III of England and II of Scotland (1650–1702). Son of the Prince of Orange who married Mary, elder daughter of James VII, and became King when she became Queen of Scotland after accepting the offer of the throne in 1689.

Witt, Jan de (1625–72). Dutch statesman and leading opponent of the house of Orange. He and his brother were hacked to pieces by a pro-William mob in Holland.

INTRODUCTION

Wake! Scotland from thy long lethargic dream,
Seem what thou art, and be what thou shalt seem.

— 'CALEDONIA' —

Long before he wrote *The Life and Strange Surprizing Adventures of Robinson Crusoe* (1719), Daniel Defoe had a few strange, surprising adventures of his own – in Scotland. While many believe that a Scottish seaman, Alexander Selkirk, was the inspiration for the novelist's most famous fictional character, and some may know that Defoe knew Scotland well enough to write a descriptive account of it in *A Tour through the Whole Island of Great Britain,* published 1724–26, only a relative few are aware that he was an English secret agent in Scotland between 1706 and 1712. He grew to like the country so well that he considered settling there with his family, but he never secured the permanent government post that would have made this possible. For much of his life (1660–1731) he retained links with Scotland – he sent his son Benjamin to Edinburgh University and had a number of business interests – but it is his large and wide-ranging writing about Scotland and Scottish affairs that this book sets out to highlight, by bringing together representative samples from his vast output.

Defoe was already an experienced intelligence-gatherer, journalist and pamphleteer when he was employed by the English Secretary of State, Sir Robert Harley, to go to Scotland just as the Scottish parliamentary debate on the Treaty of Union got underway in the autumn of 1706. His brief was to keep the English minister informed of the progress of the debate, and to promote the Union to the Scots. Defoe worked assiduously, gaining access to influential people and entry to parliamentary committees and commissions of the Assembly of the Church of Scotland. He set up a spy network soon after his arrival in the capital to keep abreast of anti-union activities elsewhere. Riots in Glasgow, treaty burnings in Dumfries and Stirling, Cameronian rallies in the south-west were all reported to him, as were the 'conspiracies' of the Jacobite underground throughout the country.

Perspective view of Parliament House
by John Elphinstone *c.* 1740, courtesy of Edinburgh City Libraries

Copies of documents he acquired through this network were often included in his regular secret reports to Harley. At the same time, he published pro-union pamphlets, often in response to anti-union tracts, and lead articles in his periodical the *Review*, which he continued to run while based in Scotland, even publishing special Edinburgh issues for a time.

One biographer has suggested that Defoe's first visits to Scotland may have been as early as the 1690s when, following bankruptcy in 1692, he may have sought refuge there from clamouring creditors. This would

explain why he was already so well known when he made his first recorded visit to Edinburgh early in October 1706. So much so that, despite the nature of his work there, Defoe had to use his own name, although he carefully concealed the real nature of his business and used aliases in his correspondence with Harley.

A particular train of events had brought Defoe to Scotland. In 1703, he had been convicted of seditious libel and sentenced to imprisonment and public pillory for his satirical poem, *Shortest Way with the Dissenters*. Through the intervention of London-based Scot, William Paterson, founder of the Bank of England and projector of the disastrous Darien scheme, Defoe's release was arranged by Harley and the Lord Treasurer, Sidney Godolphin. Looking back in 1715, Defoe acknowledged a tremendous debt of gratitude to Harley in particular, and admitted that this had led him to offer him his services.

So began Defoe's employment by Harley, and later by Godolphin, including the Scottish assignments he himself describes as a 'special service . . . in which I had run as much risque of my life, as a grenadier upon the counterscarp'. A bankrupt again in 1706, partly because his business interests, in particular his brick and tile making works, were severely damaged during his imprisonment, employment in Scotland must have had a strong appeal, not least because of the temporary respite from creditors, some of whom pursued him until the end of his life.

His first assignment led to a stay of fifteen months, during which he sought to persuade public, parliamentary and ecclesiastical opinion of the advantages of the Union of the two kingdoms. Once the treaty passed into law in May 1707, Defoe travelled around the country. He also engaged in business, developing interests in wine wholesaling, glass manufacture and horse-trading. As early as December 1706 he had established a linen manufacture business, and soon after entered into partnership with Scottish weaver James Ochiltree to produce Union of Great Britain commemorative tablecloths.

Defoe complained that Edinburgh was 'a sharping dear place' and frequently had to remind Harley to send funds to alleviate his near destitute situation. His pleas were often ignored. He finally returned to London in

January 1708 but within months, and with only three days' notice, he was dispatched to Scotland again, this time by Godolphin (Harley had fallen from power in February). His mission this time was to report on Jacobite activity following the attempted landing of James Stuart, the Old Pretender, near Edinburgh in March 1708. In addition, Defoe was to placate Presbyterian ministers whose wavering commitment to the Union, it was feared, could benefit the Jacobite cause.

Defoe remained until November 1708, having witnessed the election of Scottish members to the new British parliament in June, and was back again between August and December the following year when he secured the rights to two Scottish newspapers, the *Scots Postboy* and the *Edinburgh Courant*. This was the same year that he finally saw the delayed publication of his *History of the Union* by the Edinburgh printer Agnes Anderson. From his surviving letters it seems that he was back in the Scottish capital in 1710 (for the election of peers in November) and then again in 1712, possibly mainly on private business, for his son Benjamin was by then enrolled at the university.

His prolific publications show that Defoe was a man of unremitting mental energy. His often arduous journeys on horseback to and from Scotland, in all kinds of weather, suggest that he must have been physically robust too. In the mistaken belief that he was dying in 1715 (he lived for over fifteen years more), he wrote 'an account of myself, and of my past conduct to the world' entitled *An Appeal to Honour and Justice*, in which he refers to the personal dangers he was exposed to as Harley's agent in Scotland, and describes his employment under Godolphin's direction as an 'errand . . . such as was far from being unfit for a sovereign to direct, or an honest man to perform'.

His honesty comes into question, however, when he goes on to claim that Harley (whom he avoids naming) 'never prescrib'd to me what I should write, or should not write in my life; neither did he ever concern himself to dictate to, or restrain me in any kind; nor did he see any one tract that I ever wrote before it was printed'. While much of this statement may be *literally* true, there is little doubt that some of his writing, notably the *Review*, was a vehicle for Harleyite propaganda, and his letters to his employer contain evidence that he did from time to time submit drafts of tracts for his approval.

Political opponents and rival journalists regularly branded Defoe as a 'hireling' or 'hired pen', especially in his promotion of the Union of the Parliaments, and later, when he infiltrated a Tory, pro-Jacobite newspaper at the government's request, he was vilified as a 'turncoat'. This seems not to have troubled him too much: after all, as he tells us himself, he had already been publicly vilified as a 'villain, rascal, miscreant, lyer, bankrupt', by people motivated, he liked to counter, by 'party-malice', or political partisanship.

It is probably fair to say that Defoe protests rather too much for a man who can be caught in the act of lying about his reasons for being in Scotland, as when he claims, for instance, in his *History of the Union* (1709) that simple curiosity and the encouragement of friends prompted him to go to Edinburgh in time for the start of the Treaty debate in October 1706. A year later, when he had been there so long that suspicions were rife, he attempted to deflect these by arguing rather disingenuously in the *Review* that if he were a hired mercenary then it was surely strange that 'I have not yet had one penny of my wages, nor the least consideration for my time spent in this service'. There are grains, but only grains, of truth in these claims. He may not have been on the government payroll, but he was reimbursed for most of the expenses he incured as a secret agent from Harley's personal purse, often belatedly as already noted.

Defoe enjoyed subterfuge. He likened himself to Cardinal Richelieu on one occasion, and on another he boasted to Harley about the web of deceit he was spinning:

I flatter myself you will have no complaint of my conduct. I have faithful emissaries in every company, and I talk to everybody in their own way, to the merchants I am about to settle here in trade, building ships &c., with the lawyers I want to purchase a house and land to bring my family and live upon it. God knows where the money is to pay for it!

Today I am going into partnership with a member of Parliament in a glass house; tomorrow with another in a salt work, with the Glasgow mutineers I am to be a fish merchant, with the Aberdeen men a woollen, and with the Perth and Western men a linen manufacturer, and still at the end of all discourse the Union is the essential, and I am all to everyone that I may gain some.

(Letter to Harley, 26 November, 1706)

No doubt Defoe thought the end justified the means. As he says here, 'the Union is the essential'. Concealment of his real purposes was, of course, vital for his own protection. The chilling words of his friend and pro-Unionist, John Clerk of Penicuik, make this perfectly clear: he was 'a Spy amongst us, but not known to be such, otherways the Mob of Edinburgh had pulled him to pieces' (*Memoirs of the Life of Sir John Clerk*).

Yet to leave the impression that Defoe was an unprincipled rogue who deceived friends and enemies alike would be misleading. He was a man who held a number of firm convictions throughout his long and eventful career. Raised as a dissenter from the established Church of England, from an early age he was committed to the Protestant, Hanoverian Succession and frequently declared his aversion to the mainly Catholic or Episcopalian, Jacobite cause. He seems to have been genuinely concerned about the dangers to the throne of Great Britain and to the security of the Presbyterian Church of Scotland that Scottish Jacobites in particular presented. From time to time he presented himself as Scotland's champion, and it seems that he really did believe that 'poor Scotland' could only benefit from the Union with England, through greater civil and religious liberties, a settled succession, and an established church whose security was protected under the Act of Union. In his *Tour of Scotland* which was published late in his life, he expressed disappointment that his hopes and predictions about what Scotland would gain from the Union were not all realised.

In view of the nature of his work, Defoe considered himself lucky to be alive at the end of his first Scottish mission 'in spite of Scotch mobs . . .

---

bullying Jacobites' and 'mad' Glasgow men, but nevertheless he seems to have developed a real liking for the country and people. Indeed, he was vexed to find when he returned much later as a tourist that so many Scottish towns had not made the most of their post-Union opportunities in trade and commerce. As someone who spent around eight out of every twelve months in Scotland over a period of six years, he gained considerable insight into what the people thought about some of the momentous issues of the day. It was an eventful period, and his informed commentaries on the political, economic, religious and social scene make interesting reading. Nevertheless, his standpoint is always that of an outsider, an Englishman, and he had enough reminders of this at the time, whether as a potential target for the Edinburgh mob in 1706, or as a tourist finding a cool reception in Angus in the 1720s. There is some dispute about the extent of his actual influence on events in Scotland at the time, most notably the Union he advocated so vigorously. At the very least – and this was no small thing – through his pamphlets, *Review* and *History of the Union* he helped enlighten other English men and women whose general ignorance about Scotland was often remarked at the time, while the clandestine activities he engaged in at an English government's bidding, revealed in his secret letters, left to posterity a glimpse of what went on behind the scenes.

This book introduces and presents a wide selection of Defoe's writing on Scotland and Scottish affairs, covering politics – the Union and the Jacobite challenge – in chapters one and two; trade and agriculture in chapter three; religion in chapter four; and Scots and Scotland in chapter five. While Defoe's original spelling is retained, I have adopted modern conventions for punctuation and capitalisation for all primary sources. When citing Defoe's letters, *Colonel Jack* and the *Review Review'd*, I have accepted each respective editor's practice.

CHAPTER 1

Witness to the Union

For there's, no Doubt, a Juncture, when
Nations go mad as well as men
– 'Hymn to a Mob' –

Ever since the Union of the Crowns in 1603, a union of the parliaments of Scotland and England had been likely, if not inevitable[1] Ironically, it was because relations between the two countries had worsened that a closer union came to be seen as the only solution. The massacre of Glencoe in 1692 (discussed in chapter 5) and the Darien disaster in 1699 (see chapter 3) were bitterly resented in Scotland. For their part, the English were aggrieved by the execution of the captain and the crew of the *Worcester* after the English vessel moored in the Firth of Forth in 1704.

The crisis over the succession when Queen Anne ascended the throne in 1702 without an heir only deepened when the English parliament passed an act (1703) settling the succession on the House of Hanover when Anne died, while the Scottish parliament passed the Act of Security (1704) which provided for a different successor to the throne of Scotland unless the 'liberty and trade of the nation' were secured. The English retaliated with an act declaring all native Scots 'aliens', thus preventing them from holding property in England or importing and exporting Scottish produce. A weakened Scottish economy and a strong desire to get into the lucrative overseas trade England enjoyed finally convinced the Scottish parliament that a closer union was desirable. Influential Scotsmen like the Duke of

Queensberry, the Earls of Cromarty, Mar, Roxburgh and Stair, the latter's brothers Sir David and Sir Hew Dalrymple, and Sir John Clerk of Penicuik, promoted the union. Proposals for a confederated or limited union that would allow the Scots to retain a separate parliament gave way under pressure from England for a fully incorporated union. In the spring of 1706, thirty-one Scottish Commissioners went to London to negotiate with their English counterparts, and by 22 July had agreed a treaty of twenty-five articles which were brought before the Scottish parliament for debate in early October. Growing opposition among the Scottish public – according to one estimate three out of every four Scots were against it, many on account of the anticipated rise in taxes and customs – led to mob protests in Edinburgh and Glasgow.

The extracts below come from Defoe's secret correspondence with the English minister Robert Harley, his propaganda pamphlets and his journalism.

DEFOE'S MISSION

Part of his special Scottish mission instructions from Harley have survived, and it is clear from these that in his role as an undercover agent Defoe was required to provide a weekly report and to promote the Union among the Scots at every opportunity.

1. You are to use the utmost caution that it may not be supposed you are employed by any person in England, but that you came there on your own business and out of love to the country.
2. You are to write constantly the true state how you find things, at least once a week, and you need not subscribe any name but direct for me under cover to Mrs. Collins at the Posthouse, Middle Temple Gate, London. For variety you may direct under cover to Michael Read, in York Buldings.

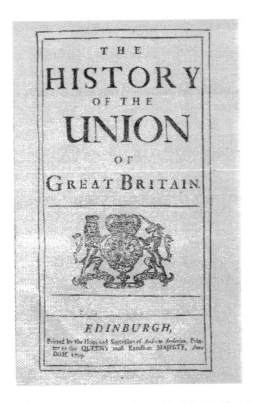

Title page from Defoe's *History of the Union of Great Britain* (Edinburgh, 1709).
Alexander Turnbull Library, Wellington, New Zealand (SPC-03-597)

3. You may confidently assure those you converse with that the Queen and all those who have credit with her are sincere and hearty for the Union.

4. You must shew them this is such an opportunity that being once lost or neglected is not again to be recovered. England never was before in so good a disposition to make such large concessions, or so heartily to unite with Scotland, and should their kindness now be slighted.[2]

(Instructions from Harley, September/October 1706)

Nº G*.

PROCLAMATION

Againſt Tumults and Rabbles.

ANNE By the Grace of GOD, Queen of *Great-Britain, France,* and *Ireland,* Defender of the Faith : To Our Lyon King at Arms, and his Brethren Heraulds, Macers of Our Privy Council, Purſevants, Meſſengers at Arms, Our Sheriffs in that part, conjunctly and ſeverally, ſpecially Conſtitute Greeting. *Foraſmuchas,* notwithſtanding that the raiſing of Tumults be a moſt dangerous, pernicious, and unboundable Practice, contrary to the very Being and Conſtitution of Government, and Deſtructive of the chief Ends thereof, The Safety and Security of Mens Lives and Fortunes ; And that by ſeveral *Acts* of *Parliament,* ſuch as *Ja. 2d Par.* 14. *Cap.* 77. And *Jac. 4th Par. 3d Cap* 34. It is Statute that there be no Commotion, nor riſing of Commons in Burrows, in hindering of the Common Law ; And that if any does in the contrary, and Knowledge or Tent may be gotten thereof ; *Their Goods* be Confiſcate to the King, and their Lives be at the King's Will : As alſo, by the *Act* of *Parliament Ja. 6th, Par.* 18. *Cap.* 11. It is Statute, That no Perſon within Burgh take upon Hand, under whatſomever pretext, to convocate, without the Knowledge and Licence of the Magiſtrates, under the Pain to be puniſhed in their Body and Goods, with all Rigour. As likeways, that the haill Inhabitants of the ſaid Burgh readily Aſſiſt and Concurr with the Magiſtrates for ſettling and puniſhing the ſaids Tumults, under the pain of being Foſterers and Maintainers thereof. Likeas, by the *Act* of *Parliament, Ja 6th Par.* 17, *Cap.* 4th. It is Statute, that whatſoever Perſon Invades or Purſues any of his Highneſs Seſſion, Secret Council, or any of his Highneſs Officiars : It being verified and Tryed, That they were purſued and Invaded for doing of his Highneſs Service, ſhall be puniſhed to the Death : There hath happened within theſe Few Days, and particularly on the Twenty Third Inſtant, and near to the *Parliament-Houſe,* and in the *Parliament-*

B   *Cloſs*

Royal Proclamation Against Tumults and Rabbles issued by
Edinburgh City Council on 24 October, 1706, as reproduced by
Defoe in his *History of the Union of Great Britain* (Edinburgh, 1709).
Alexander Turnbull Library, Wellington, New Zealand
(SPC-03-598)

ANTI-UNION RIOTS

The strength of anti-Union feeling in Scotland at the time comes through in Defoe's reports to Harley, most vividly in his eyewitness account of the mobs in the High Street a few weeks after his arrival in Edinburgh.[3] His fears for his own safety as an Englishman also come through loud and clear.

According to your commands in the only paper of your orders *viz.* of writing constantly to you, I continue to give you the general state of things here.

I am sorry to tell you here is a most confused scene of affairs, and the Ministry have a very difficult course to steer. You allow me freedom of speaking allegories in such a case: it seems to me the Presbyterians are hard at work to restore Episcopacy, and the rabble to bring to pass the Union.

We have had two mobs since my last, and expect a third, and of these the following is a short account. The first was in the Assembly or Commission of Assembly, where very strange things were talked of and in a strange manner, and I confess such as has put me much out of love with ecclesiastic Parliaments. . . .

But we had the last two nights a worse mob than this, and that was in the street, and certainly a Scots rabble is the worst of its kind.

The first night they only threatened hard and followed their patron Duke Hamilton's chair with huzzas from the Parliament House quite through the city – they came up again hallooing in the dark, threw some stones at the guard, broke a few windows and the like, and so it ended. I was warned that night that I should take care of myself, and not appear in the street, which indeed for the last five days I have done very little, having been confined by a violent cold. However, I went up the street in a friend's coach in the evening, and some of the mob not then got together were heard to say when I went into a house, "There was one of the English dogs, &c." I casually stayed at the house I went then to, till dark, and thinking to return to my lodging found the whole city in a most dreadful uproar and the High Street full of rabble.

Duke Hamilton came from the House in his chair as usual, and instead of going down the city to his lodgings went up the High Street, as was said, to visit the Duke of Athol. This, whether designed by the Duke as most think, or no, but if not was exactly calculated to begin the tumult, for the mob in a vast crowd attending him thither waited at the door – and as these people did not come there to be idle, the Duke could have done nothing more directly to point out their business, the late Lord Provost, Sir Patrick Johnstone, living just upon the spot.

The mob had threatened him before, and I had been told he had such notice of it that he removed himself. Others say he was in his lodgings with eleven or twelve gentlemen besides servants resolved to defend himself, but be that as it will, the mob came upstairs to his door and fell to work with sledges to break it open, but it seems could not. His Lady in the fright with two candles in her hand that she might be known, opens the windows, and cries out for God's sake to call the guard.

An honest townsman and apothecary that saw the distress the family was in, went to the guard which is kept in the middle of the street, and found the officers very indifferent in the matter, whether as to the cause or, as is rather judged, through real fear of the rabble; but applying himself to one Capt. Richardson, a brave resolute officer, he told him he could not go from the guard without the Lord Provost's order, but if he would obtain that order, he would go up. – In short, the order was obtained and the Captain went with a party of the guard and made his way through the rabble to Sir Patrick Johnstone's staircase. The generality of them fled, some were knocked down and the staircase cleared, and three or four taken in the very assaulting the door.

Yet they fled not far, but hallooing and throwing stones and sticks at the soldiers. Several of them are very much bruised and the brave Captain I am told keeps his bed. However he brought down his prisoners, and the Tolbooth being at hand, hurried them in, and made his retreat to the guard. In this posture things stood about eight to nine o'clock, and the street seeming passable I sallied out and got to my lodgings.

I had not been long there, but I heard a great noise and looking out saw a terrible multitude come up the High Street, with a drum at the head of them, shouting and swearing and crying out all Scotland would stand together, "No union!" "No union!" "English dogs!" and the like.

I cannot say to you I had no apprehensions, nor was Mons. de Witt quite out of my thoughts, and particularly when a part of this mob fell upon a gentleman who had discretion little enough to say something that displeased them just under my window. He defended himself bravely and called out lustily also for help to the guard, who being within hearing and ready drawn up in close order in the street advanced, rescued the gentleman, and took the person he was grappled with prisoner.

The city was by this time in a terrible fright, the guards were insulted and stoned as they stood, the mob put out all lights, nobody could stir in the streets, and not a light be seen in a window for fear of stones. There was a design to have shut the gate at the Nether Bow, as they call it, which is a gate in the middle of the great street, as Temple Bar may be, and the design was to hinder the guard in the city and the guard in the Canongate, as they call it, from assisting one another, and cut off their communication.

But my Lord Commissioner [4] prevented that by sending a detachment of his guards up the Canongate Street – as from Whitehall to Temple bar – who seized upon the Nether Bow and took post there with every soldier a link [5] in his hand beside his arms.

During this hurry, whether they omitted shutting the North

Port, as they call it, which goes to Leith, or that it was not yet ten o'clock I know not, but a second rabble of five hundred, some say a thousand, stout fellows came up from Leith and disporting themselves in the street continued the hurry in a terrible manner.

About eleven o'clock my Lord Commissioner sent for the Lord Provost and desired him to let him send a body of the guards into the city – which they say is what never was admitted before, and some say the Lord Provost hesitated at it for a long time. I cannot send you the particulars of that part – but about midnight a body of the guards besides those posted at the Canongate entered the city, drums beating, marched up the High Street to the Parliament Close, and his Grace the Duke of Argyle mounted at the head of the Horse Guards to have seconded them. After the foot came my Lord Provost, the bailiffs and magistrates with their officers and links, and these clearing the streets the mob was dispersed. They have six I think or thereabouts in prison, and the Council is now sitting to take some further orders for preserving the peace.

Two regiments of foot are sent for to quarter in the city, and I hope as before, this mob will, like our Tackers, be a mere plot to hasten what they designed to prevent.

What further happens in this matter I shall as it occurs not fail to acquaint your honour with.

(Letter to Robert Harley, Edinburgh, 24 October, 1706)

ADDRESSING NATIONAL PREJUDICES

Defoe confronted national prejudices directly in a series of pamphlets designed to persuade both Scots and English of the advantages of union, the first two of which, aimed at English readers, appeared before he left London. When he discovered that these were being exploited by Scottish anti-Unionists, he quickly rose to the challenge of explaining himself to the

Scots and of pressing home the benefits of an incorporating union to them. In doing so, he employed one of his favourite images – of the Union as a living being.

Having wrote two essays in England upon the subject of the Union, and particularly to remove national and party prejudices against the treaty then on foot, I calculated those essays principally for the English part, where I always expected the difficulty would lye, and where I met with certain radicated tho ill grounded prejudices against the Scots as a nation, as well as against the Union which I thought a general happiness.

But I confess my self surpriz'd when, coming to Edinburgh on some private affairs of my own, I found my two essays re-printed here, and forwardly handed about as arguments against that very subject they were written to promote, I mean the Union; and that only upon this weak supposition, that because I had only insisted upon the advantages to England in Union, that therefore I did not pretend Scotland should any way be better'd by it.

To this my answer is very short: that I had always too great a respect for the Scots to write a satyr upon the nation; and that thinking it impossible any Scotsman could be to seek in the real, numerous, and so visible advantages Scotland shall reap by the treaty, I thought it would seem to reflect too much upon the gentlemen concern'd to presume to tell them what it was much better manners for me to presume they all knew already, and what by the nature of the thing became so visible, that to me it seem'd none but the willfully blind, whom I do not pretend to cure, could be at a loss about.

But since it is my misfortune to be thus mistaken, and that some people charge me with that ignorance which my respect for their understanding would not permitt me to charge them with, I find my self oblig'd, contrary to my fixt resolution of not medling on either side, to make this short essay on the respective advantages of Scotland in the depending Treaty of Union. . . .

Really, gentlemen, when I wrote those essays, I conceiv'd them of use to Scotland, to convince some unbelieving Englishmen that your great advantages should be no injury to them. It was a loud and continued cry there, "Ay, ay, we know the Scots will gain by this Union; but what shall we, we in England, be the better for it?" And I was challeng'd often to make out what the English should gain by it.

Upon this I undertook that subject, and really there lies some unhappiness in the alternative of this matter; and an impartial writer, as I hope I may pretend to be, has a great difficulty before him in urging the advantages of either nation, since the arguments to prove the advantages of one, seem to argue the disadvantages of the other. . . .

I liken this Union to a body receiving food, as flesh, fish, fruit, liquids, &c., all which, being incorporated and digested, concoct together, unite their very substance and dissolve themselves into one and the same nutriment to the health, life, vigour and growth of the whole body, proportionedly and universally.

If wrong digestion, distemper of the body, or defect of the food produces corruption, contagion or improper fermentation, the most remote member and the nearest or more immediate equally feel their proportion'd want of nourishment, decay of strength, distemper and disorder; the deficiency cannot be felt in the head and not in the foot, but weakness succeeds to all the parts.

If our Union be partial, federal, periodical or indeed notional, as most of those schemes have been, then the defects may be so also: one part may thrive, and another decay; and Scotland would be but too sensible of that, in those sorts of union.

But if the Union be an incorporation, a union according to the extent of the letter, it must then be a union of the very soul of the nation, all its constitution, customs, trade and manners, must be blended together, digested and concocted, for the mutual united, undistinguish't, good, growth and health of the one, whole, united body; and this I understand by Union.

In trade, the united riches, stocks, settlements, factories, and dependencies of England are concern'd to promote yours, not as their sister-Scotland, but as their own riches, stocks in trade, &c; not in a separate but an immediate capacity. Their ports are yours, and you are immediately naturalized to, and legitimated in, their custome-houses, ports and commerce. Your manufactures are carried to them, and what you want imported from them, without taxes, tolls distinction or interruption . . .

'Twould be worth your considering the advantages of introduceing English improvements on your estates, and perhaps English farmers and stocks on your lands, the exportation of your corn and coals to English mercats; and whether it will not be your own fault if these things do not in a few years double the fee simple, and raise the value of your estates two for one.

Your lands enclosed, manured and cultivated, would be as rich, your cattel as large, your sheep as fat, and your wool as fine as in England. Your barren muirs would yield corn, the hills feed flocks of sheep, and your better lands, which you now wholly imploy with the plough, would feed strong and valuable cattel; from hence would proceed darys, milk, butter, cheese &c., which being plentiful and cheap would feed your poor in a better manner, and deliver them from the misery and hardship which now makes your people fly from their native country, and makes you the nurses of Europe, that you have the trouble and expense of your children till they are grown up, and then other nations reap the profit of their labour.

And here I must own, I am astonisht that any one can help seeing the safety, settlement and perpetuity of the establisht Church of Scotland, entirely wrapt up in the Union, and indeed only to be secured by it. . . .

'Tis for ever rendered impossible to overthrow the settlement of the Presbyterian Church of Scotland, but by subverting the constitution, by absolute arbitrary government and the openest bare-fac'd tyranny. The Church and the constitution, the spiritual and temporal liberty, have the same sanction, subsist and depend upon the same security, are defended by the same power, demanded by the same right, twisted and connected together, cannot fall, but by the same disaster, nor stand, but by the support of one another.

In Union, love, peace, charity and mutual assistance are natural consequences.

'Tis certain as things are the Church of Scotland is far from safe; and I should be excusable if I should say nothing but miracle or a Union can make her so.

If the Church of Scotland is now in a precarious, unsafe, and unsettled condition, and may be secured by the Union, then the members of this Church, can no more ask me what they gain by the Union, nor answer it to their consciences, or their posterity, that they should oppose her Settlement in this the day of her Establishment.

"But," say the gentlemen, that in behalf of the Church argue against the Union as now proposed, "we in Scotland are not safe by the Union, for we are deprived of our Parliament, and delivered over to the Parliament of England; and we do not know but such a time may come when the Parliament of England, whose constitution is wholly Episcopal, may vote our Church down, and erect the Episcopal Church of England as the establishment of Great Britain; putting us off in Scotland with a toleration which also they may by an occasional bill reduce again to any thing they please".

This I take to be the summ and state of the question, for really, what the other party objects, in my opinion, carries with it no weight.

*(An Essay at Removing National Prejudices
Against a Union with England*, part III, Edinburgh, October, 1706)

DEFOE PLAYS HIS PART

Defoe's inside knowledge of the parliamentary debate on the articles as it proceeded through November and his own influence on parliamentary committees are conveyed in two extracts from his letters to Harley:

Since my last the face of affairs I hope is a little mended, and after a very long and warm debate on Friday whether they should proceed on the Union, or go first on the securities of the Church it was passed – proceed.

On Saturday they sat till near eight at night and the speeches on both sides were long and warm. Duke Hamilton raved, Fletcher of Saltoun, and the Earl of Belhaven made long speeches, the latter of which will be printed[6] – the clamour without was so great that a rabble was feared, though the guards are numerous, and were drawn out in readiness. . . .

Last night the grand question was put whether the first article, or in short the Union itself, should be approved or not – and carried in the affirmative, which being on King William's birthday is to me very remarkable and encouraging.

I had today the honour to be sent for by the Lords Committee for examining the equivalents, and to assist them in the calculating the drawback on the sale, the proportion of the excise, and some *addenda* about trade.

They profess themselves obliged to me more than I merit, and at their next committee I am desired to dine with them. I am looked on as an Englishman that designs to settle here, and I think am perfectly unsuspected and hope on that foot I do some service. Only I spend you a great deal of money at which I am concerned and see no remedy if I will go through with the work. I have now great hopes of it though today the Assembly men make a great stir; in short the Kirk are *au wood*, pardon the Scotticism.

(Letter to Harley, Edinburgh, 5 November, 1706)

I had this day the honour to be in the Committee of Parliament appointed to examine the drawbacks and equivalents and they have desired me to assist them. . . .

I shall in my next I hope be able to give you a scheme of their demands, and as I believe I shall have the honour to draw them out for them. I would be glad that after I send you a draft of this subject I might be instructed what will or will not be conceded in England, since it is so ordered that I am in their Cabinet by some management and can influence them more than I expected.

Next post I shall transmit a draft of the things in debate . . .

(Letter to Harley, 9 November, 1706)

CAUSE FOR CELEBRATION

When the treaty was finally passed, Defoe broadcast his sense of sheer exhilaration and personal satisfaction in a job well done in his *Review*.

I have a long time dwelt on the subject of a Union; I have happily seen it transacted in the kingdom of Scotland; I have seen it carry'd on there thro' innumerable oppositions, both publick and private, peaceable and unpeaceable; I have seen it perfected there, and ratify'd, sent up to England, debated, oppos'd, and at last pass'd in both houses, and having obtain'd the royal assent, I have the pleasure, just while I am writing these lines, to hear the guns proclaiming the happy conjunction from Edinburgh Castle.

And tho' it brings an unsatisfying childish custom in play, and exposes me to a vain, and truly ridiculous saying in England, *as the fool thinks, &c.*, yet 'tis impossible to put the lively sound of the cannon just now firing into any other note to my ear than the articulate expression of UNION, UNION. . . .

Nor am I an idle spectator here. I have told Scotland of improvements in trade, wealth and shipping, that shall accrue to them on the happy conclusion of this affair, and I am pleas'd doubly with this, that I am like to be one of the first men that shall give them the pleasure of the experiment.

I have told them of the improvement of their coal trade, and 'tis their own fault if they do not particularly engage 20 or 25 sail of ships immediately from England on that work.

I have told them of the improvement of their salt, and I am now contracting for English merchants for Scots salt to the value of above 10000 *l. per annum.*

I have told them of linen manufactures, and I have now above 100 poor families at work, by my procuring and direction, for the making such sorts of linen and in such manner as never was made here before, and as no person in the trade will believe could be made here, till they see it.

This has been my employment in Scotland, and this my endeavour to do that nation service, and convince them by the practice, that what I have said of the Union, has more weight in it, than some have endeavour'd to perswade them.

Those that have charg'd me with missions and commissions, from neither they nor I know who, shall blush at their rudeness, and be asham'd for reflecting on a man come hither on purpose to do them good.

(*Review*, Saturday, 29 March, 1707)

. . . And Suspicion

The longer Defoe stayed in Scotland, the more and more difficult if became to maintain his cover. His own writing is one of the main sources of information about the suspicions and outright accusations he incurred.

I have for a long time patiently born with the scurrilous prints and scandalous reproaches of the street concerning my being in Scotland. Today I am sent thither by one party, tomorrow by another; this time by one particular person, that by a body of people; one one way, one another. And I have long waited to see if out of innumerable guesses they would at last make the discovery of the true, and to me melancholy, reason of setting my self in a remote corner of the world, which if they had done, I should no question have been insulted enough upon that head.

But since their guesses have too much party-malice in them to be right – tho' there are 5 or 6 Persons in London who cannot only give them a true account of my removal, but recall me from this banishment, if they had humanity in them a degree less than an African lyon – I therefore cannot but take up a little room in these papers about my own case. . . .

But I come to the censures of the world – *An under-spur leather*, says one angry and raging creature, *sent down into Scotland to make the Union – sent down to write for the Union, will not the voyage of the Union bear to send the Review into Scotland, &c. and the like.* . . .

But beyond this behold two new ones – one who is pleas'd to bestow threatning language, gives me his compliment as follows.

REVIEW,
Your canting and pleading for the Union *loses all its virtue in the just reproaches you lie under, of being a hired* mercenary *sent down to* Scotland *by the Court, and directed there to write for your pay; and like a meer piece of clock-work, strike as the hand that points to you, and as the weight of reward is* screw'd *up, you have been told this by a noble lord long ago, and by several of your wretched brethren, the scriblers of the town. Expect not therefore any regard to what you say, for 'tis all lyes, forgeries* and counterfeit; *your design is to enflame and ruine*

the Church of GOD and the nation; *and therefore impudent scribler, hold thy tongue, or expect* not long to have a tongue *to blaspheme thy superiours.* . . .

How now shall I do to reconcile these three gentlemen; one says, I am sent by particular persons, another by the Court – who he means by that is not determin'd; and the third by the Presbyterians. . . .

But since you have been so very free with me about my being *sent*, let me tell you and all the world something in which I am perswaded you will be on my side; if I have been sent hither as you say, I have been most barbarously treated. The Scriptures says, *no man goes a warfare on his own expence*, and I profess solemnly I have not yet had one penny of my wages, nor the least consideration for my time spent in this service; nor had I had the good fortune to have my brains knock'd out in the High Flying mobs here, when the name of an *Englishman* imply'd one that was for the Union.

(*Review*, MISCELLANEA, Tuesday, 2 September, 1707)

RALLYING THE PEERS

Promoting the Union did not end with the passing of the Act of Union on 1 May 1707. In the lead-up to the election to the first British parliament, Defoe reminded the Scottish nobility of their responsibility to make the Union work for Scotland's benefit, as the following two extracts show.

Time, my Lords, and God's Providence has already concurred to make the Union a means of deliverance to Scotland, and it is very remarkable that God has brought this nation to a kind of necessity of giving him publick thanks for the Union; the thanksgiving on the third of June being in its nature no less, as it was a thanksgiving for a mercy received by the agency of that nation you are united to, and effected as a consequence of the Union, by virtue of which only England became obliged at their own expence to rescue you out of the hands of popery and tyranny, from which it is manifest Scotland could by no means have delivered her self.

Those that say this merits no thanks either to England, or to the Union, and renounce the obligation or sense of kindness, because England had been obliged to do it for her own safety, seem like the ungratful wretch, that when his house was on fire, would give no thanks to his neighbour that put it out, because his own interest obliged him to do it, to save his own house which was next. . . .

But in order to bring the design of this paper down to your Lordships' immediate contemplation, your Lordships are most humbly intreated to look a little into and consider the present state of your native countrey, and perhaps by this your Lordships may be helped to see how much it is in your Lordships' power, and must of necessity be your undoubted duty, to promote its settlement and prosperity.

Scotland, my Lords, promised her self, and many of your Lordships in your thoughts promised your selves for her, a great many advantages from the Union. It would be an unpleasant contemplation to offer to your Lordships, that the disappointment of all the good things Scotland might expect from the Union should lie at the door of her nobility, the sons of her triumph, which are her boast and her glory, some of whom were the very means of making this very Union, and without whom it had never been brought to perfection.

And yet so it is, and so it will appear to be, unless your Lordships shall in time consider the state of your countrey, listen to its groans, hear the voice of its circumstances, and immediately apply your selves to the proper remedies.

(*A Memorial to the Nobility of Scotland*, Edinburgh, 1708)

I have always been a foreteller of good from the Union, and have put you in hopes of much upon that head; but, gentlemen, pray remember this, and bear witness for me, I never told Britain on either hand, North or South, that the Union would do you good whether you would or no: that in spight of jarring parties, ambitious interests, unnatural strifes, and the spreading poisons of envy, party malice, and the like, the Union would make you happy.

(*Scotland in Danger*, Edinburgh 1708)

UNION AND NO UNION

Defoe's dismay at the lack of goodwill on both sides of the border and his alarm at the talk of breaking the Union within only six years of unification are evident in the final excerpts printed here. He regrets that a general lack of goodwill as well as perceived breaches of the Act of Union are undermining that very Union, but he argues nevertheless that the Union itself is indissoluble. He issues challenging questions about the consequences of breaking this vital bond, and warns of the dangers of disenchantment and the advantage this could give to Jacobites and the French. These warnings were not only timely as Queen Anne's reign drew to a close (paving the way for the Hanoverian succession) but, as the 1715 Rebellion demonstrated, were to prove all too accurate.

That the kingdoms of England and Scotland are united by an establish'd constitution and formed both into one body, now called the kingdom of Great Britain, which constitution is called the Union, this is well enough known. But that there is union little enough among us, as well about the establishment of that constitution it self as about the observing or not observing the articles made between us, is the great misfortune of both nations.

I believe I may say without giving anyone offence, that a firmer union of policy with less union of affection has hardly been known in the whole world. Nay, it will not, I believe, be offer'd or suggested that there is any visible increase of good will, charity, or love of neighbourhood between the nations since the finishing the transaction of the late Treaty of Union. I am very sorry to note a truth so little to our consolation.

1. First, matters of religion between Presbyterian and Episcopal. The breach here seems to lye thus: the Presbyterians having capitulated in the Treaty of Union for the security of their church and for the preserving all its privileges, both as to discipline and government and the uniformity also as to doctrine and worship, expected perhaps from thence that no encouragement, countenance, or protection, much less toleration, should be given to the Episcopal (called there the Prelatic) party; and therefore these, when the Act for Tollerating the Episcopal meetings was pass'd, an act for restoring the Yule vacance, and another to restore the right of patrons to presentation of ministers to vacant benefices &c, these I say, cry out loudly, "the Union was broken".

On the other hand, the Episcopal or Prelatick party, finding Her Majesty her self (being educated in the same opinion) very tender of them, the Church of England in charity embracing and espousing them, and the times as they supposed favouring them further than before, failed not to push on their interest, to press for their liberty, and unhappily to lay their hopes upon that exploded article.

2. The second head consists of state matters, or the affair of the succession between the Pretender and the House of Hanover. In these affairs the Presbyterians tho' not at all in the Jacobite interest, yet openly many of them refuse to take the abjuration, and when the same is enforced and imposed upon them under severe penalties and forfeitures, they loudly complain of that law as a breach of the Union, which Union they say (and that very

truely) stipulated that no oaths should be imposed upon them contrary to their principles; and this oath, they say, is against their principles, as it obliges them voluntarily to forswear and abjure a Presbyterian king as such, tho' otherwise his descent and birth gave him an unquestioned title to the crown. Therefore, they say the Union is broken and dissolved.

On the other hand, the Jacobite Party bringing first all their treasonable arguments to assert the just claim (as they call it) of the Pretender to the crown, affirm that such right is hereditary and indefeasible, and that no humane power can legally supersede that claim.

(*Union and No Union*, London, 1713)

Our discourse is all now about breaking the Union, and having a bill brought into Parliament for dissolving the Union. I have said enough formerly to the question, whether the Union can or cannot be dissolv'd; and I am still of the opinion, without in the least reflecting upon the Parliament, that it cannot: because, as I have always said, that power which made it is not in being, and nothing can make void a being but the power that created it.

But waving this matter, and all that has been said or done in Parliament about it, which it becomes not me to meddle with, I would in as serious a manner as possible, offer a few enquiries to those who think the Union ought to be broken and dissolv'd, which I shall speak a little to as I go on.

In what state or condition do you think, or is it probable, England and Scotland must live, I mean relating to one another and relating to peace and war, if the Union should be dissolv'd?

In what condition will both parts of the island be, as to the Protestant succession, in case of a dissolving the Union? Will the succession be stronger or weaker? Will it be better secur'd, or worse, by it?

How long do you think, or is it probable, after the dissolving the Union, would it be, before the Pretender would be proclaimed king there?

Is it possible that a man of common sense can desire the Union should be dissolv'd, and not be a traytor to the Protestant succession, and a friend to the Pretender?

What condition would the Presbyterian Church, now settled in Scotland, be in if the Union was to be dissolved? And how long would it stand?

I could offer a great many more queries of this nature; but I wish wise men would consider these a little seriously, when they talk of dissolving the Union. *There's no bearing this,* said the flownder in the frying-pan, and *out it jumps into the fire.* There may be hardships, there may be pressing taxes and burthens grievous to bear; I am very sorry for them. But they who talk of dissolving the Union for this, like the disciples whom our Saviour reprov'd, it may be said to them, *Ye know not what spirit you are of.* I presume to say, they do not sufficiently consider what dissolving the Union is, and what would follow it.

To hear a Jacobite, a Scots Episcopal man, or a non-juror say the Union is broke and ought to be declared void, I do not wonder at it at all. They are in the right of it. As Jacobites, they have no other game to play for the Pretender, but to hear a member of the Church of Scotland, that loves Liberty and the Revolution, I say, to hear him talk so, is to hear a man talk delirious and besides himself, and to suppose him many degrees worse than mad.

The questions above are not jests. Any man that looks into our state here, and the state of Scotland there, will not find them so. The powerful faction of the Jacobites, tho' it is not so strong as to be feared by England, is too strong not to be feared by Scotland – not but that the Presbyterian establish'd interest in Scotland, if well supported, and especially if well united, would be sufficient to oppose and suppress too all the power of the Jacobites among them. Mark it, I say *among them*; but if the Jacobite party are supported from abroad, who shall withstand him there? Nor are the honest people so united among themselves, which is still worse, as to be in a condition to withstand any considerable strength of foreign help, that the Jacobite interest might procure.

Farther, if Scotland were divided from England again, and her separate constitution restor'd, how far the French king will understand his present treaty to extend to a peace with the Queen of Scotland, is not for me to determine; or whether he may think himself obliged by the treaty not to assist the Pretender in setting himself up in Scotland, is difficult to answer.[7] He has ancient leagues, subsisting between Scotland and France, that may oblige him, as they did his ancestors, always to support Scotland.

(*Review*, Thursday, 4 June, 1713)

A Timely Reproach

Finally, drawing once again on his favoured metaphor of the Union as a living body, Defoe rather graphically describes an attack on any part of it, specifically Scotland, as not only a form of self-mutilation but as ultimately a kind of suicide. He goes on to employ another favourite image of the Union, marriage, and roundly criticises England for failing to keep faith with the vows made at the time of union with Scotland. He also undertakes to make what restitution he can.

Scotland being by the Union become a part of our selves, he that stabbs Scotland, may legally be said to wound himself; for a man is equally a self-murtherer what part of his body soever receives the wound, and he that shoots himself into the belly is as much *felo de se*, as he that cuts his own throat.

Scotland cannot but take it ill to be so us'd since the marriage when she reflects upon the vows made to her in the courting.

I resolve to make her amends, and silence all her complaints against her spouse, for as a son of England has affronted her, so a son of England shall do her justice, and the national quarrel will be fairly ballanc'd between us.

(The Scots Nation and Union Vindicated, London, 1714)

CHAPTER 2

The Jacobites

Expect Troubles from the North

– 'Second-Sighted Highlander', 1712 –

With the 'Glorious Revolution' of 1688-9, Catholic king James VII of Scotland and II of England was deposed and his Protestant daughter Mary and her husband William of Orange became the monarchs of the two kingdoms. The Jacobites, originally named because of their support for James (*Jacobus* is Latin for James), made a number of attempts to restore the exiled Stuart king and his descendants, James Francis Stuart (1688–1766), the 'Old Pretender', and Charles Edward Stuart (1720–88), the 'Young Pretender', to the throne. Of these, the Jacobite Rebellions of 1715 and 1745 are the most famous. There were several others. The first, in 1689, was led by Graham of Claverhouse, Viscount Dundee, who won a victory at Killiecrankie in July, only to die on the battlefield. leaving the Jacobites leaderless. Then in 1708 the Old Pretender tried to invade Scotland by sea, but when the French fleet assisting him missed the Firth of Forth because of bad weather, the planned rebellion was aborted. Insufficient support doomed the 1719 rising.

Four of these revolts, or attempted revolts, took place during Defoe's adult life. As a young man he had joined the Duke of Monmouth's rebellion against James II in 1685 and, until he died in 1731, he abhorred Jacobites, and never tired of saying so. One of the reasons he was so enthusiastic about the Union was its provision for the security of the Protestant Hanoverian Succession after the death of the last Stuart monarch, Anne (1702–14), enshrined in article two of the Act of Union. He also appreciated that significant opposition to the Union came from what he called the 'Jacobite Party' in Scotland which, although mainly Tory and Episcopalian, attracted some Presbyterian support (including the Cameronians). When the publication of his *History of the Union of Great Britain*, which was largely written in Edinburgh in 1707, was delayed until 1709 by problems at the printers, he took the opportunity to write and insert a long *Preface* in which he voiced his concern about the 1708 attempted invasion which in the meantime had taken place. The complacency of the English alarmed him, so he set about spelling out the dangers if the French had landed their forces, for he was convinced that 'they would with very little opposition have been masters of the whole country'.

EARLY IMPRESSIONS

Being in Scotland gave Defoe a heightened awareness of the dangers of Jacobitism, and he adopted a number of ways of alerting others to these. Shortly after his arrival in Edinburgh in October 1706 he ridiculed Jacobite aspirations in a *Review* article:

What an unhappy wretched sort of people are those we call Jacobites! Unhappy in that their hopes, happiness and wishes are all centred on the veriest trifle, the most unexhal'd vapour, the most unconceiv'd whymsie in nature, a confusion of nations form'd in their own imaginations, centred upon a meer nothing, an uncondens'd thought, an unrarified waterish fancy, without any manner of real foundation or sufficient parts to form a probability.

(From the *Review*, Saturday, 12 October, 1706)

ON THE CASE

Before the end of 1706, he was outlining his apprehensions to Harley about
the sudden influx of Highlanders to Edinburgh and the 'secret designs' afoot
in the capital and in the west of Scotland where, according to his spy John
Pierce, Cameronian support for the Jacobites was growing.

[U]nusual concourse of strangers and Highlanders are resorted
to town in these few weeks. At the ferries of Leith and Queen's
Ferry unusual numbers of men armed and horses have been
seen to come over, and some circular letters have been
discovered sent privately about. This makes honest people here
very uneasy, and I must own I am not without just
apprehensions.

Yesterday there was a great Council at the Abbey, and today
the Parliament met – there was no business done, but to form the
enclosed proclamation,[8] which passed not without great
opposition and a protest with a number of adherers. 'Tis certain
there are some secret designs on foot, what they are time and
Providence alone can discover.

In this critical juncture J. P[ierce] is returned. I cannot attempt
to give you the history of his journey in particular, but 'tis a most
unaccountable thing to think how the Jacobite subtlety had
imposed upon the ignorant people there and brought them to be
ready to join with almost anybody to raise a disturbance. . . .

Finly,[9] though a prisoner in the Castle, openly drinks King
James the 8th's health. . . . I leave no stone unturned in this work,
I have procured letters from some dissenting ministers in
England to Mr John Hepburn, and to some of his principal
neighbours, to qualify and persuade him, not to peace only, but
to persuade his people to the like. After all, I assure you 'tis a
very critical juncture, and things are ripening apace; it will be
either a Union or all confusion in a few weeks more. . . .

Postscript – The above was wrote yesterday, the consternation here increases and I see every honest man loaded with concern even in their countenances, they say there are above a hundred strangers come into town to-day. I have removed my lodging, for I have been openly threatened to be the first sacrifice.

(Letter to Harley, Edinburgh, 27 December, 1706)

THE 1708 RISING

In his account of the foiled 1708 rebellion Defoe warns that if the Old Pretender's invasion plan had succeeded, it would have led to a reversal of the Glorious Revolution, and would have brought England's war with France too close to home. Defoe took comfort in the fact that the abortive attempt had shown that Presbyterian anti-Unionists were not, after all, prepared to support a French-assisted invasion.

[T]he French invasion . . . endangered not the Union only, but bid fair for overturning the whole frame of the present establishment in church and state, tearing up the very foundation of our constitution, I mean the Revolution, and restoring, not only tyranny and arbitrary government, but even popery it self. . . .

On Friday March the 12th, they made the coast of Scotland, but found themselves the hight of Montross, about fifteen leagues to the north of the mouth of the firth of Edinburgh. Here they made signals, and some boats going off to them, they were informed where they were; then they stood away southward, and spent all that day before they got to the mouth of the firth.

Now they sent one ship, *viz.* the Salisbury, up the firth, whether it was to make any signal to their party, to give notice of their coming, or to get any intelligence, remains yet undetermined. They made the firth just as the tide was spent, and were therefore obliged to spend six hours more at anchor, under the Isle of Maii in the mouth of the firth, and here, on the fourteenth early in the morning, they find themselves overtaken, their scouts discovering the English fleet standing in for the mouth of the firth.

Here then, they find their enterprise at an end, their moments are gone in which they might have put their errand in execution, and now they have no more to do, but to make the best of their way to sea. . . .

It must be confest, never was nation in such a condition to be invaded and there is no doubt, but had the French landed their forces, and got their stores of arms and ammunition on shore, as they might easily have done if they had not overshot their port, they would with very little opposition have been masters of the whole country. . . . When the French were thus possest of Edinburgh, it is very reasonable to imagine that the first thing they would have done, was to proclaim their king. . . .

The first laws should be to rescind the Revolution, declare the limited succession a visible rebellion, and an invasion of the right of another – and thus a compleat national turn should have pass'd upon us – and the Revolution should suffer a re-revolution in a few weeks. . . .

All this time the French and Jacobites in Scotland would have had to have strengthened their new settlement, form'd their army, fortified Leith, and other places, and have prepared for war.

I shall readily grant as any body can desire, that when the English army came to be ready, and to enter Scotland, they should beat these new invaders out of all, and that they should in time pay dear for the attempt; but it must be granted, this would have these consequences withal: 1. that it would have ruin'd Scotland; 2. brought the seat of war home to our own doors; 3. cause a diversion of our forces, and been an occasion of withdrawing our troops from Flanders, where the enemy felt the greatest weight of the war; and 4. have exceedingly protracted the war. Those gentlemen that were for having them land, may consult these probable consequences, and they will see whether they have not very good reason to be sensible of the happiness of the disappointment. . . .

It was expected, and indeed apprehended very much in England, that those of the Presbyterians who had before vigorously appeared against the Union and profest their dislike of it upon all occasions, would have appeared against the Government at this juncture, and either have joyn'd with the invaders, or have formed a third party, and so have made a division, which had in its kind been equally fatal.

But in this also they were disappointed, for the people who were most warm against the Union, nay even the western men who do not own or join with the church,[10] yet all as one man declared against joining with French invaders, papists, and a returning tyranny, which they easily forsaw must be the consequence of an invasion.

(Preface to *History of the Union*, Edinburgh, 1709)

INSULTS AND OUTRAGE

Defoe went on to deplore the encouragement to Jacobite 'insolence' given by the Scottish judges who acquitted those charged in connection with the planned rebellion.

If you come to enquire into the numbers and the insolence of the Jacobite party, how they have escap'd from justice, and their rehearsal calling it *coming off with honour*, how they insult the government, rabble the church, affront justice, and bid defiance to law; here I readily allow, the French has rather greater encouragement than he had before; and here I wish some things were the subject of our enquiry, *viz.* how these last arraign'd there came to be acquitted and assoil'd,[11] and perhaps in such an enquiry the behaviour of the judges in criminal cases in Scotland may come to be enquir'd into, not in this case only, but some others. For if this matter be not enquir'd into, it may be found a more difficult matter to convict a Jacobite in Scotland than most people are at present aware of, and this may be a particular reason why the Jacobites there are arriv'd to such an insolence, in that they promise to themselves an easie escape, either from the defect of law or the defect of executing the law. Nor will our new Act[12] now on foot prevent this part, for if the laws pass never so many amendments and alterations, if the judges of those laws are not so chosen or so regulated as that we may arrive to a clear and impartial execution of those laws, it will be to very little purpose to have them altered.

This therefore must be allow'd to be a most material branch of our enquiry into the invasion. Whether the ways for traytors to escape punishment in Scotland, and the doors for them to fly out at, are not so many and so wide open as to give encouragement to a party to insult the Government, depending upon impunity and assoilment in case of being brought to the bar; and this enquiry is more particularly needful at this time, by how much the acquitting these men is made an argument why they should not have been taken up, which by the way, I must think, is the greatest mistake imaginable; for if the Government in such a time as this was of publick danger from an invading Pretender shall not have power to apprehend any body, but such against whom there is sufficient evidence, men of profess'd aversions to the Government shall have liberty to carry their attempts against it to a very great height, and the government shall have no power to lay hold on them, till perhaps they may be too strong to be laid hold on.

(from the *Review*, Saturday, 5 February, 1709)

COUNTER-PLOTTING

In 1710 rumours of another Jacobite plot led Defoe to propose to Harley that he should return to Scotland to gather intelligence. He even suggests that it might be a good thing if the Pretender were to come over from France as this could bring matters to a head and help identify the real extent of his support.

As to the coming of the Pretender, the vain scarecrow is too visible. I know not whether, if ever we should wish for him, it should not be now, and that an invasion might set us to rights. Then we should see the falsity of the clamours and noise of a party, and many of those who are reproached with being for him would have an opportunity to wipe off that scandal, by discovering the persons who really are so. It is true the experiment might be costly, but a knave discovered is cheap bought almost at any price. If this method be used with success, I expect next counterfeit letters and treasonable papers to be conveyed into houses, and then be searched for; letters sent and then intercepted, innocent men to be suspected, and then to be falsely accused; and all the wicked things than can be, passed for current law among us. I hope her Majesty will take a right view of these things and will protect her faithful servants. . . .

I am preparing to receive your commands and persuade myself you will agree in this that the sooner I am there the more service I may do.

(Letter to Harley, 29 September, 1710)

JACOBITE AUDACITY

When he got to Edinburgh he found many people were openly drinking the Pretender's health, and immediately wrote to tell Harley in a partially coded letter which he signed using one of his aliases, 'Claude Guilot'.

The Tories (as we call them in England) are here a differing kind of people from ours of that denomination, being universally Jacobite and so above board as to own it, in the last of which they certainly show more honesty than discretion. It is so open a thing and so much the mode of the place to own the Pretender, drink his health, and talk most insolently of his being restored, that I think it my duty to represent this to you, for her Majesty's service, and that with the greatest concern. . . .

[P]rofessed Jacobites impose upon the poor Highlanders and other people in the country who do not look for their Saviour's coming with half the assurance as they do for that of the 214 (Pretender). . . .

[P]rofessed Jacobites such as 197 (Earl Marischal), Kilsyth, Blantyre, and Hume, who are known to aim in all they do at the Pretender and whose being now chosen[13] has many ill effects here, whatever may be as to overruling them in England. I mean as to increasing the insolence of Jacobitism in the north, where its strength is far from being contemptible.

(C. Guilot to Harley, Edinburgh, 18 November, 1710)

Meanwhile, his public anti-Jacobite campaign continued in the *Review* and included the publication of a letter purported to be from Scotland describing the riotous celebrations held there on 10 June, the Pretender's birthday.

It is evident no prince in the world, no government in the world, ever treated enemies so qualified and so circumstanced with that lenity, mercy, and gentleness, as her Majesty and the present government have treated the Jacobites, especially in Scotland. . . . The Queen has not pursu'd these people with the hand of justice, and the foolish, exasperated party have the folly to think her Majesty is just such a one as themselves – that because her

Majesty has not hang'd all the Jacobites, that therefore the Queen herself is a Jacobite.

I shall say no more by way of remark, till I have referr'd you to a letter I receiv'd last post, from Scotland, the contents whereof I believe to be very true:

Mr Review,

I have little to write but a short history of our tenth of June heroes, who did signalize themselves and solemnize that day after another manner than formerly. There was a grand convention of all the Jacobites from all the corners of the country, and least their number should be observ'd and occasion some jealousie, they divided themselves into two squadrons and met under pretext of a marriage, one in the city and the other in Hermiston, 3 or 4 miles distant from the city. That in the city was a marriage of Dr Pitcairn's servant, where he and all his cabal drank the healths and caused their musicians to play the spring (tunes) of the day, *Away Whigs away*; and *The King shall enjoy his own again* &c. That marriage in the country was the servant of the Lady Alderston of the family of Hay, where acted as Master of the Feast a certain Member of —, and where the healths and the springs of the day were also drank and play'd. But at night the two squadrons met in our city, where they acted also like the heroes of the day. Several gentlemen appearing among the mob, animating and encouraging them, and obliging the people whom they met upon the streets to fall down upon their bare knees and drink the health of King James VIII, *Confusion to the Government*, and *Confusion to the Protestant Succession!* The cry of the mob was all this while, *Down with the Whiggs! Down with the Hannoverians!* A knot of Jacobites got into Arthur Read's house, the vintner's, where they had the *haut-boys*[14] playing to them all night. They kept open windows, and another knot upon the streets answer'd to them by dancing to their musick and pledging the healths of the day, as they call them; this was between two and three in the morning. The magistrates caused the whole town council, all the deacons of crafts, all the city captains, lieutenants and ensigns, and all the constables, to assemble, and the magistrates with their white rods walk'd through the streets the whole night, to keep the peace of the city; at whose appearance the gentlemen with their retinue, the rabble, always fled as fast as their feet could carry them. (This Arthur Read's house is a little below the cross, on the south side of the street.) After this these heroes with their mobbish retinue would go to the Abbey which they said was the King's own house, and there they would drink the Pretender's health. But the Abbey guard would not allow them to enter the court, and they offering to do it by force, the guards fir'd, but only blank powder which, however, made the heroes and their rabble run for it. Thus they continu'd to ramble through the streets till six of the clock the next morning. The magistrates apprehended about 18 or 20 of them and have put them into the tolbooth where they are still lying; but drop'd some gentlemen whom they also apprehended, for reasons known to themselves. To add to the solemnities of the day there was a great bonfire on the hill call'd Arthur's Seat, another in the Calton, another in Mr Semple's parish about a mile from his house. And that they might not want a bonfire extraordinary, some persons set on fire a field of whinns and broom, about four acres of ground which burnt till the next day at six of the clock in the morning: yea, some houses in the city had illuminations openly, and most part of the ships in the harbour of Leith had out their flags and streamers. And which was most remarkable, two English men of war which were in the road of Leith had out their streamers. I think they call them the *Hynd* and the *Aldborough*, in one of which there was a great deal of small shot fir'd, and at the end of the peer of Leith there was a royal standard erected with a long streamer, and above them was a crown and thistle and St Andrew's cross, and above that, in large letters, *God save K.J. the VIIIth*, and underneath, *no abjuration*. When the magistrates got notice of this they sent Bailie Cockburn, bailie of Leith, to take this standard down, which he brought to the town, and which I saw in the council chamber. He took a list also of the names of the ships, and of the masters thereof, that had out their flags and streamers in the harbour. This is a short, tho' confus'd account, how the tenth of June was observ'd in this place. Whether the Queen's servants here will represent it to the government, I know not, but this I can assure you of, that Jacobitism is more bare fac'd here than ever; and within these two years there are some thousands more Jacobites in Scotland than there were before, so that they are upon the growing hand. I know not how it is with you.

Yours, &c.

I shall make no remarks on this excellent piece of pageantry, but only tell the gentlemen Jacobites, that in thus forcing the government to prosecute them, they do the Ministry a very great service, by making it absolutely necessary to punish them in defence of the publick peace. I shall address myself to the gentlemen themselves in my next.

(*Review*, Saturday, June 21, 1712)

SEASONABLE WARNINGS

Defoe also published a series of anti-Jacobite pamphlets in 1712-13. He tried various tacks, including outright attack where he rants against complacency amongst 'Britons' and even scare tactics, impersonating a Highland soothsayer who foretells another Jacobite rising.

For God's sake Britons, what are you doing? And whither are you going? To what dreadful precipices are ye hurrying yourselves? What! Are you selling yourselves for slaves to the French, who you have conquered; to popery, which you have reformed from; and to the Pretender, whom you have forsworn? Is this acting like Britons, like Protestants, like lovers of liberty?

(A Seasonable Warning and Caution against the Insinuations of Papists and Jacobites in Favour of the Pretender. Being a Letter from an Englishman at the Court of Hanover, London, 1712)

Britain sits still, and engages not in foreign wars, by which the people obtain some ease of taxes; but civil feuds embroil us. Our bright sun shines with many spots, and all our hemisphere suffers an eclipse by the intestine quarrel among contending sides at home. Especially expect troubles from the north of various kinds.

Great talk and private attempts about March to make way for the Pretender, but that fruit is not ripe, and some who pretend to pull it before it is come to perfection make much of it fall to the ground in the shaking. Two great men fall at this time, by whom the enemy have so many the fewer friends.

(The Second-Sighted Highlander, London, 1713)

THE IRONICAL APPROACH

Defoe also used irony to convey his sentiments and to alert his readers to the dangers if the Jacobites succeed in placing the Pretender on the Scottish throne. Not only would the Union be instantly dissolved, but an independent Scotland would undoubtedly resume its 'auld alliance' with England's great enemy, France.

But we have yet greater advantages attending this nation by the coming of the Pretender than any we have yet taken notice of; and though we have not room in this short tract to name them all, and enlarge upon them as the case may require, yet we cannot omit such due notice of them as may serve to satisfy our readers, and convince them how much they ought to favour the coming of the Pretender, as the great benefit to the whole nation; and therefore we shall begin with our brethren of Scotland. And here we may tell them, that they, of all the parts of this island, shall receive the most evident advantages, in that the setting the Pretender upon the throne shall effectually set them free from the bondage they now groan under in their abhorred subjection to England by the Union, which may, no question, be declared void, and dissolved, as a violence upon the Scottish nation, as soon as ever the Pretender shall be established upon the throne.

A few words may serve to recommend this to the Scots, since we are very well satisfied we shall be sure to oblige every side there by it. The opposition all sides made to the Union at the time of the transaction of the Union in the Parliament there, cannot but give us reason to think thus; and the present scruple even the Presbyterians themselves make of taking the abjuration, if they do not, as some pretend, assure us that the said Presbyterian nonjurors are in the interest of the Pretender, yet they undeniably prove and put it out of all question, that they are ill-pleased with the yoke of the Union, and would embrace every just occasion of being quietly and freely discharged from the fetters which they believe they bear by the said Union.

Now there is no doubt to be made but that upon the very first appearance of the Pretender, the ancient kingdom of Scotland should recover her former well-known condition, we mean, of being perfectly free and depending upon none but the king of France. How inestimable an advantage this will be to Scotland, and how effectually he will support and defend the Scots against their ancient enemies, the English, forasmuch as we have not room to enlarge upon here, we may take occasion to make out more particularly on another occasion.

But it may not be forgotten here that the Union was not only justly distasteful to the Scots themselves, but also to many good men and noble patriots of the church, some of whom entered their protests against passing and confirming or ratifying the same, such as the late Lord Hav[er]sham and the right wise and right noble E[arl] of Nott[ingham], whose reasons for being against the said Union, besides those they gave in the House of P[eer]s, which we do by no means mean to reflect upon in the least in this place; we say, whose other reasons for opposing the said Union were founded upon an implacable hatred to the Scots kirk, which has been established thereby. It may then not admit of any question, but that they would think it a very great advantage to be delivered from the same, as they would effectually be by the coming of the Pretender. Wherefore by the concurring judgment of these noble and wise persons, who on that account opposed the Union, the coming of the Pretender must be an inexpressible advantage to this nation.

Nor is the dissolving the Union so desirable a thing, merely as that Union was an establishing among us a wicked schismatical Presbyterian generation, and giving the sanction of the laws to their odious constitution, which we esteem (you know) worse than popery; but even on civil accounts, as particularly an account of the P[eer]s of Scotland, who many of them think themselves egregiously maltreated and robbed of their birthright as P[eer]s, and have expressed themselves so in a something public manner. Now we cannot think that any of these will be at all offended that all this new establishment should be revoked; nay, we have heard it openly said that the Scots are so little satisfied with the Union at this time, that if it were now to be put to the vote, as it was before, whether they should unite with England or no, there would not be one man in fifteen throughout Scotland that would vote for it.

If then it appears that the whole nation thus seems to be averse to the Union and by the coming in of this most glorious Pretender that Union will be in all appearance dissolved, and the nation freed from the incumbrance of it, will any Scots man, who is against the Union, refuse to be for the Pretender? Sure it cannot be. I know it is alleged that they will lay aside their discontent at the Union, and unite together against the Pretender, because that is to unite against popery. We will not say what a few who have their eyes in their heads may do; but as the generality of the people there are not so well reconciled together as such a thing requires, it is not unlikely that such a uniting may be prevented if the Pretender's friends there can but play the game of dividing them farther, as they should do. To which end, it cannot but be very serviceable to them to have the real advantages of receiving the Pretender laid before them, which is the true intent and meaning of the present undertaking.

(*What if the Pretender should Come?* London, 1713)

OUT OF FAVOUR

Unfortunately, the ironical approach backfired and led to Defoe's arrest for promoting the Jacobite cause, which was particularly galling for someone who so often proclaimed his 'riveted aversion' to Jacobitism. His bitter resentment at being so misunderstood is evident in the next excerpt.

[O]bserving the insolence of the Jacobite party, and how they insinuated fine things into the heads of the common people of the right and claim of the Pretender, and of the great things he would do for us if he was to come in; of his being to turn a Protestant, of his being resolved to maintain our liberties, support our funds, give liberty to Dissenters, and the like; and finding that the people began to be deluded, and that the Jacobites gain'd ground among them by these insinuations, I thought it the best service I could do the Protestant interest, and the best way to open the people's eyes to the advantages of the Protestant succession, if I took some course effectually to alarm the people with what they really ought to expect if the Pretender should come to be king. And this made me set pen to paper again.

In order to detect the influence of Jacobite emissaries as above, the first thing I wrote was a small tract call'd *A Seasonable Caution*.

Next to this, and with the same sincere design, I wrote two pamphlets, one entituled, *What if the* Pretender *should come?*; the other, *Reasons against the Succession of the House of Hanover*. Nothing can be more plain than that the titles of these books were amusements in order to put the books into the hands of those people who the Jacobites had deluded, and to bring the books to be read by them. . . .

It is certain the Jacobites curs'd those tracts and the author, and when they came to read them, being deluded by the titles according to the design, they threw them by with the greatest indignation imaginable. Had the Pretender ever come to the throne, I could have expected nothing but death, and all the ignominy and reproach that the most inveterate enemy of his person and claim could be suppos'd to suffer . . . What a surprise it must be to me to meet with all the publick clamour that informers could invent, as being guilty of writing against the Hanover succession, and as having written several pamphlets in favour of the Pretender.

No man in this nation ever had a more riveted aversion to the Pretender, and to all the family he pretended to come of. . . . For these books I was prosecuted, taken into custody, and oblig'd to give eight hundred pounds bail. . . .

Wherefore I thought it was my only way to cast my self on the clemency of her Majesty, whose goodness I had had so much experience of many ways, representing in my petition that I was far from the least intention to favour the interest of the Pretender, but that the books were all written with a sincere design to promote the interest of the house of Hanover, and humbly laid before her Majesty, as I do now before the rest of the world, the books themselves to plead in my behalf, representing farther, that I was maliciously inform'd against by those who were willing to put a construction upon the expressions different from my true meaning, and therefore, flying to her Majesty's goodness and clemency, I entreated her gracious pardon. . . .

As nothing in the world has been more my aversion than the society of Jacobites, so nothing can be a greater misfortune to me than to be accus'd and publickly reproach'd with what is of all things in the world most abhorr'd by me, and [that] which has made it the more afflicting is that this charge arises from those very things which I did with the sincerest design to manifest the contrary.

(from *Appeal to Honour and Justice*, London, 1715)

The 1715 Rebellion

It was 1715 before another rebellion was raised and Defoe's analysis, published after the Earl of Mar hoisted the Jacobite flag at the Braes of Mar in September but a month before the Battle of Sheriffmuir (13 November 1715), is a view from London, for an English audience. He avoids both over- and under-estimating the threat posed, and part of this involves de-mystifying the Highlander. He describes the clan system and how it works to promote powerful loyalties and to foster formidable warriors, but warriors who are no match for the government's better armed and disciplined army.

Our eyes are at this time wholly turn'd upon Scotland, and the discourse of the town is so engross'd by the daily accounts of the desperate resolution of the Highland clans to take up arms for the Pretender, that scarce any thing else is talk'd of.

As to matters of fact and the history of their proceedings in this unnatural case, I have nothing to do with it; our daily papers will be careful enough to inform us of every thing as it passes. But my present affair is to set right the notions of our people on one side, as well as on the other, particularly as to the ability these Highlanders have, or have not, to give us disturbance, and what we have to fear from them; and this I think, is an information we very much want. . . .

Let us not flatter ourselves then, or fright ourselves, but let us endeavour to come to a right view of the case, that we may from thence make a right judgment. Any one may see the design is laid very deep, the Jacobites have not been idle, neither has the success of their secret management been small; and were there success in the publick part of their appearing to answer their diligence, we should have more cause to dread them than I hope we shall ever have here. . . .

However, it is not talk that will remove King George from the throne; he is not to be sung out of the nation with a *Lille-burlero*,

Landing of James Stuart, the Old Pretender, at Peterhead (1715)
by P. Schenk, courtesy of the Scottish National Portrait Gallery

as King James was; and therefore to encourage ourselves in the just defence of the king and kingdom, let us enquire boldly into the strength of the enemy and not be afraid to make the most of it.

The insurrection is at present only in the Highlands of Scotland; it is indeed threatned in other places, but there only they are yet actually in arms. Nor will I suppose here that they will be able to make head in any other places. The vigilance of the government, and the power that they have at hand to suppress them being considered, we have great reason to hope they will not; and as it is not for any faithful subject to say what rebels may attempt, so neither is it fit we should intimidate or prepossess the minds of the people with apprehensions of danger, when they are rather to be encourag'd to prevent than to expect it. . . .

I find our people at a great loss to know . . . who they are to fight with, or what the manner of the war is like to be; and this ignorance leads into many errors, particularly, that on one hand they are apt to slight and contemn them as a weak and despicable people, not of consequence enough to give us any concern, not powerful enough to make any disturbance, or worth our while to raise troops against, but easily to be suppress'd by the zeal of the loyal people in Scotland, and by the ordinary militia of the county, and this I think an error which may be dangerous one way; or on the other hand, they are so terrified and allarmed at these Highlanders, as if they were all giants of the sons of Anak,[15] the most terrible fellows in the world, so dreadful for their personal valour that no men were able to match them, and so formidable for their numbers that all the forces in the nation were not sufficient to attack them, and that therefore nothing could now be done, without calling foreign forces over to our assistance. . . .

First then to the question, what these Highlanders are? Take it in a few words:

They are the inhabitants of the norwest parts of Scotland, including the midland part also, from the Water of Tay to the Water of Nesse.

But as there are other Highlanders in Scotland besides those who I am now to speak of, I desire the reader to observe that by these Highlanders I am to be understood those who are now in rebellion, for there are the western Highlands, as well as the north, and these are generally those who are subject to the family of the Campbells, of whom the Duke of Argyle is the chief or head, and to the family of Douglass, of whom the late Duke of Queensbury was a collateral branch, and the present Duke of

Douglass, a minor, is the chief. These are not at all concern'd in this rebellion, but are in many parts of a quite differing interest, and rather enclin'd to the Cameronian Presbyterians than to the Jacobite party.

Adjoining to these, and indeed the beginning of the north Highlanders are the family of *Broad-albin*; the word describes the people, *Broad* signifying in the Highland tongue greatest or most extended, and *albin* a mountain, from whence also the most mountainous part of Scotland is called Albany, or of the mountains.

These Highlanders, we are told, are in the conspiracy and that their head, who is the Earl of Broad-albin and of the family of [Campbell] is one of the peers of Scotland now in rebellion. His forces, meerly as chief of the name, are not esteemed to be above 1200 men; but as some of his neighbouring clans are to be suppos'd to receive encouragement from his example and to join their servants and vassals to his, they have reported that the Broad-albin men are 4000, which tho' I must question the truth of, yet I leave it to time to discover. . . .

Some of our accounts inform us that the rebels have extended themselves east over all the shires of Angus, Nairn, Aberdeen, the Gowrie and to the Firth of Cromarty, from Montross to Inverness and, that having the pass of St Johnstown over the Tay, they are masters of the province of Fife. I say, should this be true, then we may allow them to possess one full half of Scotland, as to extent of land I mean, but not as to the wealth, plentifulness and number of the inhabitants; nor is there any doubt but that as soon as the king's forces come to action, and to advance upon them, but they will be soon obliged to quit the Lowlands of Fife, Angus, &c. and be confin'd to a narrower compass. . . .

The manners of these people are rude and barbarous, and tho' subject to the British government, yet the common people know no laws or government but the absolute will of their chief. They are divided into clans or families, of which the eldest branch always preserves the authority, and is called their chief, and by his primogeniture demands such a homage that all the colateral lines or branches of the family are subject to him by a kind of natural law. Under these chiefs are the several gentlemen of the name, who have again under them their tenants and vassals; the first are their absolute slaves, and being scarce sensible of any other law, or of any other government, the laird or landlord commands them and their substances on all occasions. . . .

This subjection naturally allows that those chiefs have it more in their power to disturb the civil peace of the kingdom than it were to be wish'd any subjects in so well ordered a government as this is ought to be trusted with; and the present rebellion is an unanswerable proof of it, for upon this authority of the chiefs and lairds is founded the whole expectation of the Pretender. . . .

[T]hese Highlanders are more inur'd to arms than the inhabitants of any other part of Scotland, their way of living being to get their subsistance in the mountains by their gun, shooting wild-fowl, deer &c., and by this means they are not only all furnished with arms, but as they live sometimes in enmity with one another, and decide their personal breaches very often by the sword, in which sometimes from the small differences between two mean persons the whole families are engaged, and they often come to pitch'd battles, one clan against another, so it occasions them to be more acquainted with their arms, and with the discipline of war, than other men are; and it may be said of them that they are the best undisciplin'd soldiers that can be in the world; and tho' the way of our fighting in the field is of late much altered, and disciplin'd troops are become much more terrible than ever before, yet it was found by experience, at the fight at Gilly-crankey [Killiecrankie], that the raw and undisciplin'd Highlanders did, by the fury of a desperate charge, put the regular troops into confusion, and beat them out of the field; but of this I believe there is not much danger now.

The Highlander is always arm'd, the meanest man among them – even the dubscalper, a name for those who run at the horse-foot of the laird – is not without a gun, a broad sword, a durk and a target. . . .

They wear pumps for shoes, so thin as that they rather tread the ground than the shoe, and this is for their convenience in running; and by which, as has been observed of them, they have this advantage in fight, that if they are beaten there is no overtaking them, and if they conquer it is very hard to get away from them. But their sense of this nimble faculty has also some inconveniencies, which is (*viz.*), that if the impetuosity of their first charge is firmly received, and they cannot make an impression with their first shock, they think of trusting to their feet sooner than other men, and when they begin to run very seldom look behind them or rally again till they recover the top of the hills, where they are sure not to be follow'd by the horse; so that our men have nothing to do but to receive the first fury of their charge and stand firm, and they may be sure the Highlanders seldom make a second. . . .

[T]hey are wedded to . . . their way of fighting, and it is the hardest thing imaginable to bring them, I mean in their own country, to alter their method or to fall into the new discipline, or indeed to be perswaded that it is better than their own. This infirmity of their temper is as sure a pledge of their being beaten whenever they come into the field as can be desir'd, it being as impossible for them to break into a line of our men (when they stand with their bayonets on their firelocks charged as pikes). . . .

Besides, we are to take notice that the Highlanders, hurried by the impetuosity of their tempers, are far from being the most observant of their lines, and choose to fight in their open order, as it may be called, that they may have room to swing about their heavy broad and unweildy swords, which in our way of fighting are of very little use. . . . The blow is slow and must be preceded by lifting up and falling down, the thrust is swift and speedy; the blow cannot be redoubled or recovered without time, the thrust is recovered and redoubled in a moment. In a word, the soldier can make three thrusts to one blow. From all which I infer that the antient terror of these Highlanders is entirely vanish'd, and that unless the Earl of Mar who now leads this rebellious and barbarian army can alter their way of fighting, which he will find very difficult to do, our new way has so much the advantage of them that the King's army will be able to fight them tho' they were three for one.

(*A View of the Scots Rebellion*, London, 15 October, 1715)

Touring Perth, Glamis Castle and Sheriffmuir

We also have the view of Defoe the tourist who visited places associated with the '15 some years afterwards. In particular, he observes that Perth has benefited economically from the quartering of first Jacobite and then government forces there during the rising. He imagines the special arrangements that must have been made to accommodate the Pretender and his retinue when they were billeted at Glamis Castle. His visit to the Sheriffmuir battlefield provokes his amazement that Mar's 'rabble of Highlanders' had so nearly defeated the government troops.

Perth

This town was unhappily for some time the seat of the late rebellion, but I cannot say it was unhappy for the town: for the townsmen got so much money by both parties, that they are evidently enriched by it; and it appears not only by the particular families and persons in the town, but by their publick and private buildings which they have raised since that, as particularly a new tolbooth or town-hall. . . .

It seems a little enigmatick to us in the south, how a rebellion should enrich any place, but a few words will explain it. First, I must premise that the Pretender and his troops lay near or in this place a considerable time. Now the bare consumption of victuals and drink is a very considerable advantage in Scotland, and therefore 'tis frequent in Scotland for towns to petition the government to have regiments of soldiers quartered upon them, which in England would look monstrous, nothing being more terrible and uneasy [to] our towns in England.

Again, as the Pretender and his troops lay in the neighbourhood, namely at Scone, so a very great confluence of the nobility, clergy, and gentry, however fatally as to themselves, gathered about him and appeared here also, making their court to him in person and waiting the issue of his fortunes, till they found the storm gathering from the south, and no probable means to resist it, all relief from abroad being everywhere disappointed, and then they shifted off as they could.

While they resided here, their expence of money was exceeding great: lodgings in the town of Perth let for such a rate as was never known in the place before; trade was in a kind of a hurry, provision dear. In a word, the people, not of the town only, but of all the country round, were enrich'd; and had it lasted two or three months longer, it would have made all the towns rich.

When this cloud was dispersed, and all the party fled and gone, the victors entered, the general officers and the loyal gentlemen succeeded the abdicated and routed party. But here was still the headquarters, and afterwards the Dutch troops[16] continued here most part of the winter; all this while the money flowed in, and the town made their market on both sides, for they gained by the royal army's being on that side of the country, and by the foreigners being quartered there, almost as much, tho' not in so little time as by the other.

The town was well built before, but now has almost a new face; (for as I said) here are abundance of new houses, and more of old houses new fitted and repaired, which look like new.

GLAMIS CASTLE

[T]he Pretender lodg'd here, for the Earl of Strathmore entertained him in his first passage to Perth with great magnificence. There were [all] told three and forty furnish'd rooms on the first floor of the house; some beds, perhaps, were put up for the occasion, for they made eighty-eight beds for them, and the whole retinue of the Pretender was received, the house being able to receive the court of a real reigning prince. . . .

From hence I came away south west and, crossing the Tay below Perth but above Dundee, came to Dumblain, a name made famous by the late battle fought between the army of King George under the command of the Duke of Argyle, and the Pretender's forces under the Earl of Marr, which was fought on Sheriff-Moor, between Sterling and Dumblain. The town is pleasantly situated and tolerably well built, but out of all manner of trade, so that there is neither present prosperity upon it, or prospect of future.

Going from hence we took a full view of the field of battle call'd Sheriff-Muir, and had time to contemplate how it was possible that a rabble of Highlanders, arm'd in haste, appearing in rebellion, headed by a person never in arms before, nor of the least experience, should come so near to the overthrowing an army of regular disciplin'd troops, and led on by experienced officers, and so great a general. But when the mistake appear'd also, we bless'd the good protector of Great Britain who, under a piece of the [most] mistaken conduct in the world, to say no worse of it, gave that important victory to King George's troops, and prevented the ruin of Scotland from an army of Highlanders.

(A Tour Through the Whole Island of
Great Britain, London, 1724-6)

IN THE CHEVALIER'S SERVICE

Finally, in his fiction, Defoe has a last fling at the Jacobites. He makes the criminal narrator of his novel, *Colonel Jack*, relate how, in the course of his adventures and despite his dubious credentials, he was readily accepted as an officer in the Chevalier's army and accompanied him on the 'fruitless expedition' from France to Scotland in 1708. He also makes his suspicion of the French king Louis XIV's motives in protecting and assisting the Pretender very clear: England was still at war with France at the time. Defoe excelled at authenticating details, so it comes as no surprise to find that his fictional account of the failed invasion agrees in the main with contemporary Scottish, English and French accounts, although it differs in the interpretation.

[T]he French king meditating nothing more than how to give the English a diversion, fitted out a strong squadron of men-of-war and frigates, at Dunkirk . . . and the new king, as we called him, though more generally he was called the Chevalier de St George, was shipped along with them, and all for Scotland. . . .

I was very well received by the Chevalier, and, as he had an account that I was an officer in the Irish brigade, and had served in Italy, and consequently was an old soldier, all this added to the character which I had before, and made me have a great deal of honour paid me, though at the same time I had no particular attachment to his person, or to his cause. . . .

[I]t belongs very little to my history to give an account of that fruitless expedition, only to tell you that, being so closely and effectually chased by the English fleet, which was superior in force to the French, I may say that, in escaping them, I escaped being hanged.

It was the good fortune of the French, that they overshot the port they aimed at, and intending for the Frith of Forth, or, as it is called, the frith of Edinburgh, the first land they made was as far north as a place called Montrose, where it was not their business to land, and so they were obliged to come back to the frith, and were gotten to the entrance of it, and came to an anchor for the tide; but this delay or hinderance gave time to the English, under Sir George Bing, to come to the frith, and they came to an anchor, just as we did, only waiting to go up the frith with the flood.

Had we not overshot the port, as above, all our squadron had been destroyed in two days, and all we could have done had been to have gotten into the pier or haven at Leith, with the smaller frigates, and have landed the troops and ammunition; but we must have set fire to the men-of-war, for the English squadron was not above twenty-four hours behind us, or thereabout.

Upon this surprise, the French admiral set sail from the north point of the frith, where we lay, and, crowding away to the north, got the start of the English fleet and made their escape, with the loss of one ship only.

(*Colonel Jack*, 1723)

CHAPTER 3

Trade and Agriculture

Fitted for Commerce and cut out for Trade
The Seas the Land, the Land the Seas invade

– 'CALEDONIA' –

Among the Scottish pro-unionists, including those who favoured a federal rather than an incorporating union, improved trade was a strong motivation. In the decade before the Scottish parliament began debates about the pros and cons of a union, the Scottish economy had been hard hit by a series of bad harvests. Poverty was rife. A major attempt to expand overseas trade through the founding of the 'Company of Scotland Trading to Africa and the Indies' had ended in the Darien disaster (1699-1700) with the loss of a great deal of money, nearly 2,000 lives, and the hopes of many more. The Alien Act (1705) prevented Scottish merchants in England from importing Scottish goods. George Scott was one of these, and he was responsible for introducing Defoe, as someone who 'understood trade & the interest of nations very well', to Scottish commissioners who came to London in April 1706 for the Treaty of Union negotiations. They persuaded Defoe to write his first pro-Union pamphlets addressing national prejudices, and may indeed have been among the friends who, he later claimed, encouraged him to go to Scotland later that year when the Scottish parliament met to debate the Treaty Articles.[17]

Defoe's own mercantile interests were varied and quite often unsuccessful, but for him the true merchant was an adventurer, one who was prepared to take risks. He took enormous pride in English manufacture and trade, both foreign and domestic, and argued that if Scotland would only emulate England in both respects, and take advantage of the opportunities the Union offered, her economy and trade would vastly improve. Trade was certainly a key union issue: more than half of the articles in the Act of Union relate to trade and the associated customs and tax provisions.

ADDRESSING ENGLISH PERCEPTIONS OF THE SCOTTISH ECONOMY

The English, too, had to be persuaded of the advantages of uniting with 'poor, barren Scotland', so within weeks of arriving in Edinburgh in October 1706 Defoe advised his English readers in the *Review* that Scotland was 'worth uniting with'.

But pray, gentlemen, what can you expect out of Scotland? Poor, barren Scotland where you fancy there is nothing to be had but wild men and ragged mountains, storms, snows, poverty and barrenness! Very well, gentlemen, and what if you should be mistaken now, and I should tell you that Scotland is quite another country than you imagine, and not so ill worth uniting with as you think; that it is a noble country, fruitful in soil, healthy air, seated for trade, full of manufactures by land, and a treasure great as the Indies at their door by sea; that the poverty of Scotland, and the fruitfulness of England, or rather the difference between them, is owing not to meer difference of the clime, heat of the sun or nature of the soil, but to the errors of time and the misery of their constitution?

To go a little farther, I am of the opinion, with some few exceptions to circumstances of foreign trade, had the liberty, justice and constitution of England been first planted and preserv'd in the north of Britain, the tyranny, cruelty and bondage of Scotland under which she has so long groaned, been the fate of the south, all that is fruitful, pleasant, rich and strong had been there; and all that is poor, barren, miserable and neglected had been here.

(*Review*, MISCELLANEA, Saturday, 19 October, 1706)

PERSUADING THE SCOTS ~~READ~~

In the same month, October 1706, Defoe published the third of his essays against national prejudice, this one aimed at persuading the Scots of the trading advantages, the access to English 'mercats' (the Scots word for 'markets' no doubt consciously chosen by Defoe), and the opportunities of introducing English agricultural improvements to Scotland. He paints a rosy picture of post-Union Scotland as a land of plenty.

In trade, the united riches, stocks, settlements, factories, and dependencies of England are concern'd to promote yours, not as their sister-Scotland, but as their own riches, stocks in trade, &c; not in a separate but an immediate capacity, their ports are yours, and you are immediately naturalized to, and legitimated in, their custome-houses, ports and commerce. Your manufactures are carried to them, and what you want imported from them, without taxes, tolls distinction or interruption. . . .

'Twould be worth your considering the advantages of introduceing English improvements on your estates, and perhaps English farmers and stocks on your lands, the exportation of your corn and coals to English mercats; and whether it will not be your own fault, if these things do not in a few years, double the fee simple, and raise the value of your estates two for one.

Your lands enclosed, manured and cultivated, would be as rich, your cattel as large, your sheep as fat, and your wool as fine as in England; your barren muirs would yield corn, the hills feed flocks of sheep, and your better lands which you now wholly imploy with the plough, would feed strong and valuable cattel. From hence would proceed darys, milk, butter, cheese &c., which being plentiful and cheap would feed your poor in a better manner, and deliver them from the misery and hardship which now makes your people fly from their native country, and makes you the nurses of Europe, that you have the trouble and expense of your children till they are grown up, and then other nations reap the profit of their labour.

(From *An Essay at Removing National Prejudices Against a Union with England*, Part III, Edinburgh, 1706)

HERRING: A SCOTTISH BLESSING

Before 1706 was over, Defoe was also using verse to encourage the Scots to take full advantage of natural resources, such as herring. He deliberately makes an appeal to the Scots' sense of pride in their country and heritage, even using the ancient name of 'Caledonia' to promote the idea of a return to greatness based on enterprise and full exploitation of the divine gift of herring.

> *Hail Caledonia*, by vast Seas embrac't;
> Those Seas for Glory, Wealth and Terror plac't.
> Dreadful in Fame, to thee familiar grown,
> Suited to no mens Temper like thy own. . . .

> Then *Caledonia* lend an humble Ear,
> And your own *ill accepted Blessings* hear,
>   From the profound unmeasur'd Deeps
>   Where Nature all her Wonders keeps.
> Her *Handmaid Instinct*, this Blest Message gave
> To all the Watry Crew beneath the Watry Cave.

Go Numberless and spread the Finny Sail,
And find Britannia Nature's Darling Isle;
There spread your Scaly Squadrons, *and submit,*
Your Makers Law Commands, To Every Net.
Be You Their Wealth *and plenteously supply*
What Coldest Soil and Steril Climes *deny.*
Be You Their Envy'd Blessing, *and attend*
The willing Prey, and to the undustrious Hand,
In proper Squadrons all your Troops divide,
And visit Every Creek, *with* Every Tide.
Present your selves to every Hungry Door,
Employ The Diligent, *and feed* The Poor.
If they reject the Bounties of the Sea
Bid 'em Complain no more of Poverty.
Upbraid their sloth, and then return to me,
    Visit no other Port.

The punctual well instructed Fish obey,
And *Scaly Squadrons* spread the Northern Sea,
Directly point their Course, and find the Shore,
    As if they'd all been here before.
Their equal Distance keep, divide and join,
Their strong Detachments send to every Creek,
In just Proportion their own Mischiefs seek.
Seek out the Harbours, seek the Indented Shore,
As if they're taught by Book, or steer'd by Line:
T'imploy the Diligent, and feed the Poor.
    No other Port they visit.

Ah! *Caledonia,* mark the High Command,
And mark the Caution of the Heavenly Hand;
If thou reject the Bounties of the Sea,
    No more Complain of Poverty.
Hadst thou in early time with Wisdom grac't
Heav'ns Bounty, as in Duty bound, embrac't,

Above the Nations thou hadst rais'd thy Head,
At Home their Envy, and abroad their dread,
Thy Wealthy Clime would all the World invite,
    They'd Court Thee to Unite.
No more of Barren Hills and Seas complain,
Reproach the Land with Blasts, with Storms the Main.

    Not all the Spicy Banks of *Ganges* Stream,
Not Fruitful *Nile* so oft the Poets Dream,
Not Isles of Pearl, not rich Pacifick Seas,
    Not the more Fruitful *Caribees*,
    Not *Africks* Wealth or *Chilean* Stores,
The *Silver Mountains*, or the *Golden Shores*,
Could such an Unexhausted Treasure boast,
    A Treasure *how supinely lost*!
What Pains has *Scotland* taken to be Poor,
    That has the *Indies* at her Door;
That lets her *Coursest Fate* of Choice remain,
And sees her Maker *Bountiful in Vain*.

    When *Caledonians*, when will you be wise,
And search for *certain Wealth* in Native Seas?
A Wealth by Heav'n design'd for *none but You*,
A Wealth that does your very Hands pursue,
Upbraids You with Neglect of Your own Right,
And courts *Invading Neighbours in your Sight*.

    When *Caledonians*, when will You be wise?
When from Your Clouded Circumstances rise?
Banish Invaders, *Heav'n's own Gifts* enjoy,
This would Your N*ative Poverty* destroy.
This would restore Your Ancient dear bought Name,
This, *and Your Valour*, would revive Your Fame.

(from Caledonia, Part I, Edinburgh, 1706)

OVERSEAS TRADE ✕ READ

The development of Scotland's overseas trade and plantations as both a desirable goal in itself and as a way of finding post-Union taxes less burdensome, is promoted by Defoe in his fifth essay aimed at *Removing National Prejudices Against a Union with England*, published in the Scottish capital in October 1707, five months after the Act of Union was passed.

The short scale of the trade from Scotland to the West-Indies consists in these heads, which when they are right stated, I shall think 'tis easy for any body to determine whether that trade is to be carried on to the advantage of Scotland, yea or no:

First, what you carry out is entirely, if you please, the product of your own land and the labour of your own people.

2. What you bring home may, at least ³⁄₄ parts of it, be again exported by you to foreign parts, and the product by consequence return to you in money; and if the remaining ¹⁄₄ part is expended at home, 'tis expended in the room of those goods of the same kind, which you now buy with your money in England, or with your goods at a short advance, and which would otherwise return you money.

3. What goods you carry out to the colonies are generally sold there at the extravagant advance of 100 per cent profit on the continent, and if for loss on the islands, then great quantities of bullion are return'd home for them, in the return of which the loss is less in proportion.

4. All this trade shall be carried on in your own ships, furnished with your own provisions, built if you please in your own ports, and manned with your own seamen.

I allow Scotland is, and has been, under discouragement both as to foreign trade and manufactures. I allow your poor are very low and your rich men backward to launch out.

But on this supposition, that by the increase of trade, shipping, manufactures and labour, the increase of wages and bettering the way of the poor's living would be the consequence, and then the taxes would not be equally burthensome as now. . . .

So that I think there remains only to prove that there will be an increase of trade: I think I have perform'd that in part; I shall be glad to see some other more able hand perfect my generals into particulars by schemes of profit and advantage on the returns to Scotland.

(*A Fifth Essay, at Removing National Prejudices Against a Union with England*, Edinburgh, 1707)

THE COMPANY OF SCOTLAND AND THE DARIEN SCHEME

Defoe's admission that Scotland had been thwarted by England in previous attempts to expand her overseas markets was veiled in his fifth essay. However, in his *History of the Union of Great Britain*, written the same year but not published until two years later, he more openly examines the reasons for English opposition to the Company of Scotland (or African Company) and the steps that contributed to the failure of this Scottish scheme to found a colony and trading centre at Darien on the isthmus of Panama.

The African Company, the large commission that Company obtained, by which they seem'd to rival the English, both in their Guinea, East-India, and West-India trade, was ill relish'd by the English, who at that time were in an odd and unsettled posture as to those trades at home. And as this is not rightly understood by a great many that run round about for reasons of the English Parliament's falling upon that affair, it may not be amiss to set it in a clearer light. . . .

Whatever prospects the projectors of that Company had in their view, some of which will, I doubt, hardly bear a history, I never heard one of them pretend that either the stock to carry it on, or the market for their trade, could be found in Scotland; and from hence, with other particular objections which I believe they never debated, I pretend to say they could never really propose any rational probability of success.

The first step the Company took, was to open books for subscriptions at London, and afterwards at Hamburgh, and this was no sooner done, but the English Company took the alarm at both and obtained by their interest with the government instructions to the English resident at Hamburgh to oppose it there, which was done most effectually.

Then they, I mean the English East-India Company, applyed themselves to the English parliament, and by offering plausible reasons there soon obtained their votes against it also, and against any of the subjects of England subscribing to it; and the Scots merchants who had subscribed in England were ordered to be impeacht of a misdemeanour, tho' the parliament being near a close those impeachments dropt of course.

These things had the desired effect, for they crushed the attempt of raising a new East-India Company in these parts of the world, and the projectors then played their other game of Darien, in which they had the same unhappiness, *viz.* to put the English nation under a necessity of opposing them. . . .

But to come to the case, the Company, or rather the projectors, who had now embark'd the gentlemen in a subscription of 400,000 pounds sterling, carried on their design, and with two ships.

Men and a cargo perfectly unqualified for any kind of trade, either with English or Spaniards, set sail and landing at Darien made a settlement there, fortified themselves, and prepared to maintain it.

The Spaniards, who claim a right there, and whether that

right be disputeable or no is not the question here, immediately proceed by a double method: first, to prepare to dislodge them by force; and secondly, apply themselves to the king of England, claiming, by virtue of the treaty made with England, ratified and exchanged, that no succour should be given to the Scots from any of the English colonies in America.

This, as an express stipulation, could not be denied by the English Court, and accordingly a proclamation was exhibited by the king of England, and sent to all the English plantations, forbidding trade or correspondence with them.

I cannot help saying, had the managers of the Companies affairs had the least forecast of things, they could not but have expected all that happened here; and also might have known that, had they acted right, those proclamations could have done them no manner of damage.

Whoever has the least knowledge of the affairs of that country, and of the trade of the English colonies, must needs know that had the Scots Company who had plac'd themselves at Darien been furnish'd either with money or letters of credit, they had never wanted provisions, or come to any other disaster, notwithstanding the proclamations of the English against correspondence.

Had the Scots at Darien had any thing sufficient to encourage the traders thither, they had never wanted provisions; and as they were unprovided that way, they must have starved had there been no prohibitions at all, for they would have found few of the planters or merchants of the colonies inclined to have furnish'd them without money.

This I think clears up the case sufficiently, and therefore I shall say no more to it here. 'Tis thus far to the present purpose that this disaster of the Scots, be the fault where it will, was one of the great occasions of ill blood between the nations, while those that took all opportunities to widen our breaches on both sides continually cryed out in England, that the Scots were encroaching upon our trade, and setting up a new East-India trade; and, on the other hand, in Scotland they complained of the unnatural and barbarous treatment of the English. . . .

(From *History of the Union of Great Britain*, Edinburgh, 1709)

 SUMMARIZE ?

REMINDING THE ENGLISH OF THEIR TREATY OBLIGATIONS

As early as December 1708, Defoe saw that the Scots were not benefiting as much as was 'promis'd in your names at the time of the Union' and proceeded to remind the English of their obligation which, he adds, is in their interest too. Once again he employs one of his favoured Union metaphors to argue that the wealth of the nation depends on the health of the whole whole 'body'.

Perhaps I may come to the subject of trade in Scotland and tell you how you may make good what was lustily promis'd in your names at the time of the Union, *viz.* that England would assist Scotland in trade, and that Scotland would be improv'd by England in trade after the Union. I must allow that so much forwardness in that matter does not yet appear as I expected, and yet tho' I did not expect at the rate some people did neither, I am not out of hope as some pretend to be, that it shall not appear at all; and therefore to do my part, I shall in this paper attempt to shew you wherein the improving Scotland in trade may consist with your improving your own trade, and if I can come to tell you how you shall get by prompting Scotland to trade, I make no question, if you will not hearken to it for their sakes, you will for your own.

But I must first talk to you a little about your own affair. Trade is the life and wealth of this nation, 'tis its nobillity, its foundation, and the great mine from whence its wealth has sprung. Whenever our commerce dies, the Common-wealth will languish; government choak'd with obstructions will have the green-sickness, grow pale and faint, and by degrees fall into an irretrievable consumption. Trade is the animal spirit to this great body which, having passed thro' many decoctions, is at last arriv'd to a moral capacity of enlivening the whole frame.

(*Review*, Saturday, 18 December, 1708)

DEFOE PROPOSES A NAVAL BASE ON THE FIRTH OF FORTH

In line with doing his part as an Englishman, Defoe came up with some specific projects in 1710 which he sent to Robert Harley, who was by then Prime Minister. The first is a far-sighted proposal to build a naval base on the Firth of Forth for the fitting and repair of ships. (Two centuries later Rosyth was erected.) He argued that this would be good for the Scottish economy because British government investment would be necessary and the Scots would experience new training and employment opportunities, better wages and a boost to business generally. There would be a consequent increase in the import and export trade and greater protection for that trade, especially important given the dangers of French invaders and pirates.

The Proposal
The short of my proposal is to erect a yard with docks, store houses, launches, wayes and the like for building, laying up, fitting and repairing of ships in Scotland, such as is now at Plymmouth, Portsmouth &c. for the use of the Navy and then to appoint a certain squadron of her Majesty's ships to have their winter station and be laid up there. . . .

That at some proper place in the Firth of Forth (and I am not to seek for the place) a yard may be erected with dry docks for repairing launches for building, and wayes for graving[18] and washing the men of war.

That offices and store houses be built for laying up and securing the sails, rigging, ammunition &c. for the said ships with victualling offices for provisions that they may be entirely fitted out to sea.

That naval stores be furnished from the proper countries and sufficient quantities laid in for all occasions.

That rope walks and all necessaries be built and provided for making all sorts of cables and cordage with encouragemts for planting timber and hemp, flax &c. for supplies.

In short, that all things be modelled according to the usage of the navy for the effectual furnishing and supplying about fourteen men of war of the fourth and fifth rate, or as many as the governmt shall appoint, and for building or rebuilding as occasion may require.

And above all that it may be in such a place in the Firth as, if possible, may be secured from the insults of an enemy and in particular as cannot be bombarded, for which proposals shall be offered when needful.

Of the Advantages of this to Scotland

It would be very long to enter into all the particular advantages, but without enlarging on the heads, they will be such as these.

1. The expending and circulating a very great sum of money every year in Scotland, and especially in the first erecting the yards.
2. The employing a great number of people in the necessary works constantly attending an undertaking of such consequence, such as carpenters, caulkers,[19] labourers &c., about the repairing and building ships, carvers, painters, joiners, blockmakers, anchorsmiths, ropemakers and a multitude of trades which depend upon the fitting out ships.

3. The breeding [of] seamen and encouraging them to stay at home in Scotland, of which a certain number would be always entertained in pay, and the youth of Scotland would have a kind of school to initiate them into the needful arts of building and navigating ships, the said men of war being always manned from Scotland.

4. Increase of shipping and trade for importing the naval stores for these things, and increase of business for goods to export.

5. Consumption of provisions, increase of wages to the poor, increase of labour and by consequence detaining the people at home, and by all these improving the land.

6. Security to the trade of Scotland in time of war. Such a strength being kept at their own doors as will be always able to protect them from pirates and sea robbers, whereas at this time there is not a gun can be fired at an enemy in all the Firth. But all the shipping there lies exposed to every rover, and it seems something wonderfull that in all this war the French have not swept the whole Firth and even burnt the very town of Leith, which they might frequently have done but with two men of war and a bomb ketch. . . . [20]

The Advantages of the Firth for Laying Up the Ships

1. For at least eight miles in length from the narrow passage as high as Alloway, the seat of the Earl of Mar, the channel is safe, the ground good, landlocked from storms, and safe for riding the ships.[21]

2. There is a full depth of water from six fathoms to eighteen fathoms at low water, for the breadth in most places of a mile so that the ships have room to wind upon the flood and ebb and ride clear of one another in case of fire.

3. A small charge will fortify the mouth of the passage at the Queen's ferry, the island of Inchgarvie lying in the middle, and the main channel not half a mile broad on either side yet deep and safe, in some places thirty to forty fathom water, so that no ships can pass but must come under the command of the batteries on both sides.

4. No enemy can come near to bombard them, or to burn the store-houses and yards, unless they bring a land force to go on shore and march round.

Thus the work will be better done and all the charges saved.

(Letter to Harley, 5 September, 1710)

USE   SEE P 95

PROPOSED NAVIGATION OF THE FORTH AND CLYDE

This proposal came to him as he toured around Scotland and became convinced that a canal linking the Firths of Forth and Clyde would be a huge advantage to commerce and trade, allowing ready movement of goods and manufactures within Britain and imported from overseas, particularly the Americas. Once again Defoe was far-sighted. It was another 42 years before work began on the Forth-Clyde canal, and another 22 before it was opened (1790).

The two firths, from the Firth of Clyde to the Firth of Forth, have not an interval of above twelve or fourteen miles which, if they were join'd, as might easily be done, they might cross Scotland, as I might say, in the very centre.

Nor can I refrain mentioning how easy a work it would be to form a navigation, I mean a navigation of art from the Forth to the Clyde, and so join the two seas, as the king of France has done in a place five times as far, and five hundred times as difficult, namely from Thouloze to Narbonne. What an advantage in commerce would this be, opening the Irish trade to the merchants of Glasgow, making a communication between the west coast of Scotland and the east coast of England, and even to London itself; nay, several ports of England on the Irish Sea, from Liverpool northward, would all trade with London by such a canal. It would take up a volume by itself to lay down the several advantages to the trade of Scotland that would immediately occur by such a navigation, and then to give a true survey of the ground, the easiness of its being performed, and the probable charge of it, all which might be done. But it is too much to undertake here; it must lye till posterity, by the rising greatness of their commerce, shall not only feel the want of it but find themselves able for the performance.

(from *A Tour of the Whole Island of Great Britain*, London 1724-6)

U S E

Observing Improvements on his Tours of Scotland

In his *Tour of Scotland* Defoe takes every opportunity to praise post-Union improvements wherever he finds them. He contrasts good progress in the west of Scotland with poor progress in the east, although there are exceptions in both cases. Dumfries is full of entrepreneurial merchant-traders shipping to England and English plantations and is compared to Liverpool and Manchester in this respect, whereas Kirkcudbright (which he spells as he heard it pronounced, 'Kirkubry') fails to exploit its fine harbour and river for trade. He even claims that the salmon 'come and offer themselves, and go again'. He blames poverty and the indolence it breeds for this failure, not lack of industry. He admires the religious sobriety he finds in the west, manifest in the swift punishment dealt out to anyone who dares to swear in public.

Glasgow is extolled as a 'city of business' taking full advantage of the Union, especially in the Americas trade. A canal linking to the east coast would be a great addition and enable trade to London and Europe, but even as things are, he says, the 'Glasgow men' have outstripped the Edinburgh merchants, although he concedes that Leith makes the most of its port. Otherwise, towns and villages on the east coast from Dunbar to Aberdeen, have not developed their full potential, especially given the plentiful supply of herring. He was nevertheless impressed by the skills of the Queensferry boys he saw catching herring with their bare hands.

Wherever he travelled in Scotland, Defoe saw room for improvement, especially in farming techniques. The one place he cannot fault in this respect is Inverness which, having a naturally fertile soil and an early harvest, gets wheat to the Edinburgh markets before the local crop is ready. He gives the greatest credit for this, however, to English expertise, introduced by those soldiers from Cromwell's army who had settled in this area. Decades later they have also influenced the language spoken there so much that it is not only the best English in Scotland but such 'perfect English' that some reckon it rivals London English. Defoe refuses to go quite so far.

THE WEST COAST

Here, indeed, as in some other ports on this side the island, the benefits of commerce obtain'd to Scotland by the Union appear visible; and that much more than on the east side, where they seem to be little, if any thing mended, I mean in their trade.

Dumfries was always a good town, and full of merchants. By merchants, here I mean in the sense that word is taken and understood in England (*viz.*) not mercers and drapers, shop keepers &c., but merchant adventurers who trade to foreign parts, and employ a considerable number of ships. But if this was so before, it is much more so now; and as they have (with success) embarked in trade, as well to England as to the English plantations, they apparently encrease both in shipping and people. For as it almost every where appears, where trade increases, people must and will increase; that is, they flock to the place by the necessary consequences of the trade and, in return, where the people increase, the trade will increase, because the necessary consumption of provisions, cloats, furniture, &c. necessarily increases, and with them the trade.

This is such a chain of trading consequences, that they are not to be separated; and the town of Dumfries, as well as Liverpool, Manchester, Whitehaven and other towns in England, are demonstrations of it.

Galloway, which is a great and rich province, promotes the trade of Dumfries very much.

Galloway, as I hinted before, begins even from the middle of the bridge of Dumfries; the first town on the coast of any note is Kirkubright or, as vulgarly called, Kirkubry. It must be acknowledged this very place is a surprize to a stranger, and especially one whose business is observation, as mine was.

Here is a pleasant situation, and yet nothing pleasant to be seen. Here is a harbour without ships, a port without trade, a fishery without nets, a people without business; and that which is worse than all, they do not seem to desire business, much less do they understand it. I believe they are very good Christians at Kirkubry, for they are in the very letter of it, they obey the text, and are contented with such things as they have. They have all the materials for trade, but no genius to it; all the opportunities for trade, but no inclination to it. In a word, they have no notion of being rich and populous, and thriving by commerce. They have a fine river, navigable for the greatest ships to the town-key; a haven, deep as a well, safe as a mill pond; 'tis a meer wet dock, for the little island of Ross lyes in the very entrance, and keeps off the west and north west winds, and breaks the surge of the sea, so that when it is rough without, 'tis always smooth within. But, alas! there is not a vessel that deserves the name of a ship belongs to it; and though here is an extraordinary salmon fishing, the salmon come and offer themselves, and go again, and cannot obtain the priviledge of being made useful to mankind, for they take very few of them. They have also white fish, but cure none; and herrings, but pickle none. In a word, it is to me the wonder of all the towns of North Britain, especially being so near England, that it has all the invitations to trade that nature can give them, but they take no notice of it. A man might say of them, that they have the Indies at their door, and will not dip into the wealth of them; a gold mine at their door, and will not dig it.

It is true the reason is in part evident, namely, poverty: no money to build vessels, hire seamen, buy nets and materials for fishing, to cure the fish when it is catch'd, or to carry it to market when it is cured; and this discourages the mind, checks industry, and prevents all manner of application. People tell us that slothfulness begets poverty, and it is true. But I must add too, that poverty makes slothfulness, and I doubt not were two or three brisk merchants to settle at Kirkubry, who had stocks to furnish ships and boats for these things, they would soon find the people as industrious and as laborious as in other places; or, if they did not find them so, when they felt the benefit of it, tasted the sweet of it, had boats to fish, and merchants to buy it when brought in; when they found the money coming, they would soon work. But to bid men trade without money, labour without wages, catch fish to have them stink when they had done, is all one as to bid them work without hands, or walk without feet; 'tis the poverty of the people makes them indolent.

In a word, the common people all over this country, not only are poor, but look poor; they appear dejected and discouraged, as if they had given over all hopes of ever being otherwise than what they are. They are, indeed, a sober, grave, religious people, and that more, ordinarily speaking, than in any other part of

Scotland, far from what it is in England. Conversation is generally sober, grave. I assure you they have no assemblies here, or balls; and far from what it is in England, you hear no oaths, or prophane words in the streets; and, if a mean boy, such as we call shoe-blackers, or black guard boys, should be heard to swear, the next gentleman in the street, if any happened to be near him, would cane him, and correct him, whereas in England nothing is more frequent, or less regarded now, than the most horrid oaths and blasphemies in the open streets, and that by the little children that hardly know what an oath means.

But this we cannot cure, and, I doubt never shall; and in Scotland, but especially in this part of Scotland, you have none of it to cure.

GLASGOW

Glasgow is [a] city of business. Here is the face of trade, as well foreign as home trade and, I may say, 'tis the only city in Scotland at this time that apparently encreases and improves in both. The Union has answered its end to them more than to any other part of Scotland, for their trade is now formed by it; and, as the Union opened the door to the Scots in our American colonies, the Glasgow merchants presently fell in with the opportunity; and tho', when the Union was making, the rabble of Glasgow made the most formidable attempt to prevent it, yet now they know better, for they have the greatest addition to their trade by it imaginable; and I am assured that they send near 50 sail of ships every year to Virginia, New England, and other English colonies in America, and are every year increasing.

Could this city but have a communication with the Firth of Forth, so as to send their tobacco and sugar by water to Alloway, below Sterling, as they might from thence again to London, Holland, Hambrough, and the Baltick, they would (for ought I

Prospect of the Town of Glasgow from the south,
courtesy of Glasgow City Libraries

know that should hinder it) in a few years double their trade,
and send 100 sail or more. . . .

As Scotland never enjoy'd a trade to the English Plantations
till since the Union, so no town in Scotland has yet done any
thing considerable in it but Glasgow. The merchants of
Edinburgh have attempted it, but they lye so out of the way, and
the voyage is not only so much the longer but so much more
hazardous, that the Glasgow men are always sure to outdo them,
and must consequently carry away that part of trade from them,
as likewise the trade to the south and to the Mediterranean,
whether the ships from Glasgow go and come again with great
advantage in the risque, so that even in the insuring there is one
per cent. difference, which is a great article in the business of a
merchant.

INVERNESS

All the country on the west side of the Spey is surprisingly agreeable, being a flat, level country. . . . The harvest in this country, and in the vale of Strath Bogy and all the country to Inverness, is not only forward and early, as well as rich and strong, but 'tis more early in [the][22] north than in Northumberland, nay, than it is in Darbyshire, and even than in some parts of the most southerly counties in England. . . .

As a confirmation of this, I affirm that I have seen the new wheat of this country and Innerness brought to market to Edinburgh before the wheat at Edinburgh has been fit to reap; and yet the harvest about Edinburgh is thought to be as forward as in most parts, even of England itself. In a word, it is usual for them to begin their harvest in Murray and the country about it in the month of July, and it is not very unusual to have new corn fully ripe and thresh'd out, shipp'd off, and brought to Edinburgh to sale, within the month of August. . . .

The town and fortress of Inner-Ness, that is a town on the inner bank of the River Ness. The situation of it, as I have said before, intimates that it is a place for strength; and accordingly it has a castle, founded in antient times to command the pass; and some authors write that it was antiently a royal house for the kings of Scotland. Be that as it will, Oliver Cromwell thought it a place of such importance that he built a strong citadel here, and kept a stated garrison always in it, and sometimes more than a garrison, finding it needful to have a large body of his veteran troops posted here to preserve the peace of the country, and keep the Highlands in awe, which they did effectually all his time.

Here it is observed that at the end of those troublesome days when the troops on all sides came to be disbanded, and the men dispersed, abundance of the English soldiers settled in this fruitful and cheap part of the country, and two things are observed from it as the consequence:

1. That the English falling to husbandry and cultivation of the earth after their own manner were instrumental, with the help of a rich and fruitful soil, to bring all that part of the country into so good a method and management as is observed to outdo all the rest of Scotland to this day; and this not a little contributes to the harvest being so early and the corn so good, as is said above, for as they reap early, so they sow early, and manure and help the soil by all the regular arts of husbandry, as is practised in England and which, as they learnt it from England and by English men, so they preserve the knowledge of it, and also the industry attending it and required for it to this day.

2. As Cromwell's soldiers initiated them thus into the arts and industry of the husbandman, so they left them the English accent upon their tongues, and they preserve it also to this day; for they speak perfect English, even much better than in the most southerly provinces of Scotland; nay, some will say that they speak it as well as at London, tho' I do not grant that neither. It is certain they keep the southern accent very well, and speak very good English.

They have also much of the English way of living among them, as well in their manner of dress and customs, as also of their eating and drinking, and even of their dressing and cookery, which we found here much more agreeable to English stomachs than in other parts of Scotland; all which, and several other usages and customs, they retain from the setting of three regiments of English soldiers here, after they were disbanded, and who had, at least many of them, their wives and children with them. . . .

All the country beyond this river, and the loch flowing in it, is call'd Caithness, and extends to the northermost land in Scotland.

Some people tell us they have both lead, copper, and iron in this part of Scotland, and I am very much inclin'd to believe it. But it seems reserv'd for a future. . . . This part of Scotland may no longer be call'd poor, for such a production would soon change the face of things, bring wealth and people and commerce to it, fill their harbours full of ships, their towns full of people and, by consuming the provisions, bring the soil to be cultivated, its fish cur'd, and its cattle consum'd at home, and so a visible prosperity would shew itself among them.

THE EAST COAST

Defoe's various missions frequently took him to Edinburgh so he was very familiar with the journey along the east coast of Scotland after crossing the border. He describes the route in his *Tour of Scotland* (see chapter 5) and the following extracts provide his observations on the economic capacities of some east coast towns, Kirkcaldy, Leith and Dunbar.

KIRKCALDY

East of this town [Kinghorn] is Kirkcaldy, a larger, more populous, and better built town than the other, and indeed than any on this coast. Its situation is in length, in one street running along the shore from east to west for a long mile, and very well built, the streets clean and well pav'd; there are some small by-streets or lanes, and it has some considerable merchants in it, I mean in the true sense of the word merchant. There are also several good ships belonging to the town. Also, as Fife is a good corn country, here are some that deal very largely in corn, and export great quantities both to England and Holland. Here are great quantities of linnen shipp'd off for England; and as these ships return freighted either from England or Holland, they bring all needful supplies of foreign goods; so that the traders in Kirkcaldy have really a very considerable traffick, both at home and abroad.

There are several coal-pits here, not only in the neighbourhood, but even close to the very sea at the west end of the town and where, one would think, the tide should make it impossible to work them. At the east end of the town is a convenient yard for building and repairing of ships, and farther east than that several salt-pans for the boyling and making of salt.

Kirkcaldy is a member of the royal burroughs, as are also Bruntisland, Kinghorn, and Dysert, tho' almost all of them together are not equal to this town, so that here are no less than four royal burroughs in the riding of five miles.

LEITH

I must now visit Leith, the sea port of Edinburgh, as it is properly called. It is a large and populous town, or rather two towns, for the river or harbour parts them and they are joined by a good stone bridge, about half a mile or more, [at] the mouth of the river.

Up to this bridge ships of burthen may come and at high water lay their sides close to the shore; but at low water people pass over on foot, even without the pier, but the water flows in the firth near three fathom right up and down.

Here is a very fine key, well wharf'd up with stone and fenced with piles, able to discharge much more business than the place can supply, tho' the trade is far from being inconsiderable too. At the mouth of the harbour is a very long and well built pier, or head, which runs out beyond the land a great way and which defends the entrance into the harbour from filling up with sand, as upon hard gales of wind at north east would be very likely. There are also ranges of piles, or break waters as the seamen call them, on the other side the harbour, all which are kept in good repair, and by this means the harbour is preserved and kept open in spight of a flat shore and a large swell of the sea.

Leith, tho' it has a particular bayliff, is yet under the jurisdiction of the magistrates of Edinburgh and is governed by them. The town had a great disaster a few years before the Union, by a storehouse of gunpowder taking fire, which demolished almost a whole street of houses; the loss is not fully repaired to this day. Many lives also were lost and many people miserably hurt and bruised which, I think, should serve as a hint to all governments not to suffer quantities of powder to be kept in populous towns.

From Leith, the firth which is there at least two leagues over, holds that breadth for five or six miles, and then narrows a little beyond Cramond and again at the Queens Ferry it is reduced to two miles breadth, and an island in the middle also.

There is also a ferry at Leith, the boats going from Leith to Burnt-Island or, as the Scots call it, Brantillian; but as 'tis no less than seven miles, and that sometimes they meet with bad weather, the passengers are so often frighted that I knew several gentlemen that would always choose to go round to the Queens Ferry rather than venture over at Leith. This, I suppose, gave beginning to that homely piece of proverb poetry that,

There is never a laird in Fife,
But once a year he would give his estate for his life.

Queens Ferry is not a passage over the water only, but a very good town also and a corporation. And here I must take notice of a thing which was so surprising, I mean as to the quantity of herrings taken, and that might be taken in those seas. There was at that time a fleet of between seven and eight hundred sail of Dutch busses come into the firth loaden with herrings, and their convoy with them, for it was in the time of the late wars. The Scots themselves had taken a vast quantity, for they said they had had a very good fishery along upon the coast of Fife and of Aberdeen, and the Dunbar men and the firth boats were every day taking more, and yet the water of the firth was so full of fish that passing at the Queens Ferry in a little Norway yawl or boat rowed by two boys, the boys toss'd the fish out of the water into the boat with their naked hands only.

DUNBAR

This town of Dunbar is a handsome well-built town upon the sea-shore, where they have a kind of a natural harbour, tho' in the middle of dangerous rocks.

They have here a great herring fishery, and particularly they hang herrings here, as they do at Yarmouth in Norfolk, for the smoking them; or, to speak the ordinary dialect, they make red herrings here. I cannot say they are cur'd so well as at Yarmouth, that is to say, not for keeping and sending on long voyages, as to Venice and Leghorn, though, with a quick passage, they might hold it thither too. However, they do it very well. The herrings also themselves may a little make the difference because they are generally larger and fatter than those at Yarmouth, which makes it more difficult to cure them so as to keep in a hot country, and on a long voyage.

The greatest thing this country wants is more enclos'd pastures, by which the farmers would keep stocks of cattle well fodder'd in the winter, and which furnish good store of butter, cheese, and beef to the market, but would, by their quantity of dung, enrich their soil according to the unanswerable maxim in grazing that stock upon land improves land.

Two other articles would encrease and enrich them, but which they never practice:

Folding their sheep;
Fallowing their plow'd land.

The first would fatten the land, and the latter destroy the weeds; but this is going out of my way. They have, indeed, near the sea, an equivalent which assists them exceedingly, namely, the sea weed. They call it the sea ware, which the sea casts up from about November to January in great quantities, and which extremely fattens and enriches the lands, so that they are plow'd from age to age without laying fallow. But farther from the sea, and where they cannot fetch it, there they are forced to lay the lands down to rest when, as we say in England, they have plow'd them out of heart, and so they get no advantage by them; whereas could they, by a stock of cattle, raise a stock of muck, or by folding sheep upon them mend them that way, and lay them down one year in three or four, as we do in England, the lands would hold from one generation to another.

But at present, for want of enclosures, they have no winter provision for black cattle; and for want of that winter-provision, the farmers have no daries, no butter or cheese; that is to say, no quantity, and no heaps of dung in their yards to return upon the lands for its improvement, and thus a good soil is impoverished for want of husbandry.

I saw here something of a manufacture and a face of industry, and it was the first that I had seen the least appearance of in Scotland. Particularly here, was a woollen manufacture, erected by a company or corporation, for making broad cloths, such as they called English cloth. And as they had English workmen employed and, which was more than all, English wool, they really made very good cloth, well mixed and good colours. But I cannot say they made it as cheap, or could bring it so cheap to market, as the English; and this was the reason that, tho' before the late Union, the English cloth being prohibited upon severe penalties, their own cloth supplied them very well, yet as soon as the Union was made, and by that means the English trade opened, the clothiers from Worcester and the counties adjoining such as Gloucester and Wilts., brought in their goods and, underselling the Scots, those manufactories were not able to hold it.

However, as I said, here was a woollen manufacture, and the people being employed in spinning, dying, weaving &c., they turned their hands to other things; and there is still some business going on to the advantage of the poor. Also upon the Tyne, near Haddington, we saw very good fulling mills; whether they still have employment, I am not certain. They talked also of setting up a paper-mill after the Union, the French paper being not allowed to be imported as formerly.

(from *A Tour of the Whole Island of
Great Britain*, London, 1724-6)

CHAPTER 4

Religion

Scotland, for whose Presbyterian Grandeur
you have a particular Veneration
− 'Review', Thursday, 14 July, 1709 −

By the Revolution Settlement (1689-90), the Presbyterian Church of Scotland was fully restored, Episcopacy was abolished, and with it the system of patronage by which lay patrons had the right to present ministers to ecclesiastical benefices. This left a number of Scots discontented. Not surprisingly, Episcopalians were unhappy about their displacement as the national church and some saw in the Jacobite cause the chance to redress the situation. Also disaffected were the Cameronians, radical Covenanters who followed field preacher Richard Cameron (d. 1680), and rejected the Revolution Settlement. Both groups saw themselves as persecuted and yet found common ground with Presbyterians who opposed the Union of Scotland with England.

Defoe recognised the importance of reconciling the Church of Scotland to the Union, and a recurrent refrain in his writing, and no doubt in the discussions he had with Scottish ministers, was that by the Union the Presbyterian Church was confirmed as the established national religion and there was no need to fear for the security of the church in an incorporated Britain. As a Protestant who was raised as a dissenter from the Church of England, Defoe certainly inclined towards the Presbyterian Church or, as he quickly came to call it, the Kirk of Scotland, but his patience was often tried as we can readily see, for example, when he writes to Harley that 'The Kirk are *au wood*, pardon the Scotticism', and later expands on this: 'the parsons here are unaccountable people, humourous, jealous, partial, censorious, haughty, insolent, and above all monstrously ignorant'. He also hoped that Episcopalians and Cameronians could be reconciled to the Union too, not least because he believed that their grievances were exploited by Jacobites. But while he regarded the Cameronians and other extreme Covenanters like the followers of John Macmillan (1669-1753) as a 'poor rash people' who merited compassion, he came to believe that the Episcopalians and Jacobites were 'but one party and one people in Scotland' whose purpose was the destruction of the Union as well as the disestablishment of the Presbyterian church.

CHAMPIONING THE CHURCH OF SCOTLAND

In his missions to Scotland, both in the lead-up to the Act of Union and subsequently, Defoe set about persuading the Presbyterians that the Union was in their interest, while at the same time he tried to enlighten Dissenters in England who, he argues, have been thoroughly misled about their Scottish brethern. When he came to write his *Memoirs of the Church of Scotland* (1717) he claimed that Scottish Presbyterians had been slandered by their enemies and he set the record straight by describing how they were the first Scots to welcome William of Orange on his arrival in England and to petition the Convention of Estates (comprising lords, prelates and representatives of the burghs of Scotland) to offer him the crown.

Whoever enquires narrowly into the subject I am now entring upon, I mean the Church of Scotland, will find it a meer *terra incognita*, a vast continent of hidden, undiscovered novelties and will find himself surprised to the last degree that things so near us should be so entirely hid from us.

Not that there is any thing monstrous or unheard of in the constitution or circumstances of this church, much less in her profession and practise, but that she has been represented to the world in so many monstrous shapes, drest up in so many devil's coats and fool's coats, charg'd with so many heresies, errors, schisms, and antichristianisms by the mob of this slandering generation, that when a man comes to view her in her original reformation, her subsequent settlement, her many revolutions, convulsions and catastrophes; in her subjected, persecuted state and now in her glorious restoration and establishment; nothing can be more wonderful in humane affairs than to see how mankind has been imposed upon about her, and with what front the absurdities charg'd on her could be broach'd in the world. . . .

Now it was seen and made plain to the world that the suffering people in Scotland acted upon no principles of enthusiasm, blind zeal or religious frenzy, as their enemies suggested; that they were no enemies to monarchy, civil government, order of society, and the like, as had been scandalously said; but that they kept strictly to the rule of God's word, adher'd to an honest cause, and acted upon just principles. . . .

This is evident by their practice at the Revolution in that no sooner was the Prince of Orange landed in England, and the enemies of our constitution began to stagger, but these people immediately took arms, and successfully chas'd the bloody party out of their country. . . . They were the first men in Scotland that address'd or petition'd the Convention of Estates to place the crown of Scotland on the head of their deliverer King William, which was done accordingly, to the restoring of religion, healing the breaches of Scotland and the utter confusion of their persecutors . . . and, upon King William's establishing their antient liberty, and that Episcopacy was depos'd, as we shall see presently they appeared to be all one united body of Presbyterians, one church, under one religious government and administration, the same in opinion, the same in doctrine, discipline, worship, and government, having fewer breaches, fewer divisions, fewer fallings off to a differing opinion, than any Protestant church in the world.

(from *Memoirs of the Church of Scotland,*
in four periods, Part I, London, 1717)

PRESBYTERIAN OPPOSITION TO THE UNION

Defoe's initial impressions of the Presbyterian opposition to the Union when he arrived in Scotland in October 1706, and of the work he would have to do to bring them around, are conveyed in his reports to Harley. He tells how he has no sooner persuaded some of these ministers than they revert to their anti-Union position, and how he resorts to employing spies when the General Assembly meets. Even on the eve of the Act of Union he fears that Scottish ministers have the power and influence 'to ruin the peace of the nation'.

Letter 1

In the Assembly or Commission of Assembly . . . very strange things were talked of and in a strange manner, and I confess such as has put me much out of love with ecclesiastic parliaments. The power, *Anglice*[23] tyranny, of the Church was here described to the life, and *jure divino* insisted upon, in prejudice civil authority; but this was by some tumultuous spirits who are overruled by men of more moderation, and, as an Assembly they act with more wisdom and honesty than they do in their private capacities, in which I confess they contribute too much to the general aversion which here is to the Union; at the same time they acknowledge they are unsafe and uneasy in their present establishment. I work incessantly with them, they go from me seemingly satisfied and pretend to be informed, but are the same men when they come among their parties – I hope what I say to you shall not prejudice them. In general they are the wisest weak men, the falsest honest men, and the steadiest unsettled people ever I met with. They mean well, but are blinded in their politics, and obstinate in opinion.

(Letter to Harley, Edinburgh, 24 October, 1706)

Letter 2

There is an entire harmony in this country, consisting in universal discords, the churchmen in particular are going mad, the parsons are out of their wits, and those who, at first, were brought over, and, pardon me, were some of them my converts, their country brethren being now come in, are all gone back and to be brought over by no persuasion.

The mob you have heard of are affrighted with the loss of the Scots Crown,[24] and the parsons maliciously humour it, and a country parson who preached yesterday at the High Kirk before the Commissioners took this text: "Behold I come quickly; hold fast that which thou hast, that no man take thy crown." He pretended not to mean an earthly crown, but made his whole sermon a bald allegory against the Union. I confess I had patience to hear him, but to an exceeding mortification.

(Letter to Harley, Edinburgh, 29 October, 1706)

Letter 3

I have not wrote so constantly as usual having nothing material to communicate, but private bills in Parliament, horse races at Leith, fire in the city and such things, which are not worth disturbing your thoughts with. To tell you that my Lord Hopetoun's horse won the plate, that a fire burnt three or four houses and five people, that the parliament have been busy about a quarrel between the doctors and surgeons (knaves all!) to determine which shall have the greatest privilege to kill people and be paid for it. These things will be so far from informing you that they will not so much as divert you. Indeed should I tell you the story of ecclesiastic frenzy in these parts and draw a scheme of north country bigotry, I could make you merry in spite of your most serious concern for the public peace.

I find there is bigotry without popery, and God's priests ride upon God's people as well as the inferior clergy of less pure churches. Certainly the clergy here have more to account for than in other places, where the customary slavery of other nations is inverted but is every jot as fatal as there. The priests lead aside silly women, these silly women more silly men; the women are the instructors, and the men are mere machines wound up just as the spring goes at home. Thus, as the velocity of motion doubles and increases as 'tis remote from its centre, so if the priest be chagrined at the Union, the good wife rails at it, and the husband grows mad. This has put a notion into my head which if ever I were to write a book should take up a good part of it. . . .

So I suppressed the book and wrote another which I call *A Short View of the State of the Protestant Religion in Britain, as it is professed by the Episcopal Church in England, the Presbyterian Church in Scotland, and the Dissenters in both.*[25] . . .

This has gotten me a complete victory and the moderate men of the clergy come every day to thank me for it. I have sent it you, enclosed by this post. . . . As I told your honour in my last my design, if you approve it, [is] to stay till I see the issue of the General Assembly, so I entreat your orders about it. I must own 'tis too much in the power of the ministers here to ruin the peace of this nation, and this makes me think the meeting of the General Assembly here a thing of more consequence than otherwise it would be at this time, and I repeat my humble motion that their session may be as short as may be. . . .

I spare no charge to carry on the work I am upon in the best manner I can, and to push the great work of reconciling the minds of the people to one another and to the Union.

To this purpose I have in the *Review*, which I humbly beg you will please to cast your eye on, begun a long series of discourses on the reciprocal duties of the two nations one to another after the Union.

In my management here I am a perfect emissary. I act the old part of Cardinal Richelieu. I have my spies and my pensioners in every place, and I confess 'tis the easiest thing in the world to hire people here to betray their friends. I have spies in the Commission in the Parliament and in the Assembly, and under pretence of writing my history I have everything told me.[26]

(Edinburgh, 18 March, 1707)

THE DEVIL OF DISTRUST

In pamphlets Defoe addressed the mutual distrust between English Dissenters and the Church of Scotland deliberately promoted, he argues, by anti-Unionists whose low tactics also include totally malicious attacks on his own good character.

I frankly own the distrust and jealousies endeavour'd to be fomented here between the Church of Scotland and the Dissenters in England is far from being the general act of the ministry, or of the most judicious of the people here; and among those many of the reverend ministers who I have the honour to converse with I find a general concern that any thing so unkind should be offer'd to them; nor shall I fail to do them all the justice, both here and in England, that I can on that head, that the spirit of distrust may spread no farther, and the innocent may not be censur'd with the guilty. . . .

'Tis mutual distrust has kept these nations so long divided and been the occasion of such seas of blood being shed between them; all the widowed families, the helpless orphans, the distrest provinces in either kingdom, for these 300 years bypast, have been principally produc'd by this monster – . This child of hell has been in every mischief, in every plot, in every war between the two nations.

To destroy this devil, this present Union is contrived. 'Tis for this all the councils of both kingdoms have been imployed; 'tis to prevent this all the enemies of our peace have struggled; and if after all the hazards run, all the tumults, rabbles and mischiefs threatned, all the endeavours of the Queen and her wisest counsellors, this part should not be obtained, all the attempts of a politick Union will be in vain. . . .

Brethren of the Church of Scotland, if the Dissenters in England are not to be trusted, whither will ye seek? What shall your temporal peace depend upon? What upholds the interest of religion in Britain but that glorious body of Protestants that, from a few years of the first Reformation, have been dayly confessors for that purity of worship which they always profest, and which you enjoy?

Why should they be distrusted that never abandon'd their cause, that never deserted the strong foundation of truth and liberty, that have defended it, and are at last built upon it in common with your selves?

The laws of Britain are their safety now, and yours also: the civil capacity is the foundation security now of your religious capacity; *magna charta* is yours by the Union as well as theirs. The great liberties of England are now laid open in common with you, a foundation so strong, so certain, so sure, that should the greatest monarchs that ever reign'd in Britain invade it, even the persecutors themselves would join with you to pull them down. . . .

Suffer a stranger to exhort you to what your own interest

ought to guide you to, and to what your experience will bless him for hereafter. . . . The gentleman that opposes me in this, shall not rally me only in print, but he shall trample me under his feet. I am content to be all that is contemptible and vile in his eyes, and in every man else, if I can but be instrumental in the least to this blessed healing temper.

I can hear him and his flatterers go about defaming my morals to lessen my argument, reproaching the man, to weaken his discourse. . . . They report me a drunkard, a swearer, a sabbath-breaker, and what not. . . . I challenge them to bring the man either here, or in England, that ever saw me drink to excess, that ever heard me swear; or in short, can charge my conversation with the least vice or immorality, with indecency, immodesty, passion, prophaneness, or any thing else that deserves reproach. When they can do this, I'll burn this book at the Mercat Cross and desire all the world to regard no more what I say.

(*A Short View of the Present State of the Protestant Religion in Britain,* Edinburgh, March 1707; second ed. London, April 1707)

CHALLENGING THE ALLEGED PERSECUTION OF DISSENTERS

Defoe risks irony for the title of one of his propagandist pamplets – *An Historical Account of the Bitter Sufferings and Melancholly Circumstances of the Episcopal Church in Scotland, under the Barbarous Usage and Bloody Persecution of the Presbyterian Church Government* (Edinburgh, August 1707) – but appears not to have been in danger of being pilloried for it as he had been in England for his *Shortest Way with the Dissenters*. This tract, aimed mainly at an English audience who had been persuaded that Episcopalians in Scotland were persecuted by the established church, presents a careful examination of the facts to show that there was actually greater toleration of dissenters in Scotland than in England. To illustrate his argument Defoe recounts how on the single occasion that Episcopalians were attacked at a meeting (probably 'a Jacobite conventicle' he adds) by a Glasgow rabble the owner of the house was so excessively compensated that 'he would be pleased to have his house rabbled once a week at the same price'.

I do confess, when I came first into Scotland I was in nothing more surprized than in the matter of the Dissenters. I had, with the generality of people in England, always believ'd, tho I had wisht it otherwise, that the Episcopal clergy in Scotland were intirely deposed and supprest, persecuted, and not permitted to keep up any form of a separation in religious matters.

And I think my self oblig'd to enter into this case, not only to do the Kirk of Scotland justice and defend her against her enemies, but to defend her against her friends. If a rake or a scoundrel ill-treat me, I think it not worth my notice, 'tis below my concern; he does it because he is a rake and a scoundrel, and the slander goes but a little way. But if a man of virtue, a man of sense, a man of religion, if a good man censures me, I am concerned at it on a twofold account: 1. Because his mistake will wound me with other good men, and make the slander be believed. 2. Because I am willing to undeceive him, and prevent his exposing himself in his reproaching me, of which, when it shall appear I am innocent, he will be ashamed, and 'tis a friendship to him to prevent his blushes.

That the Church of Scotland has carryed it with great heat and rigid severity (to put it now in the softest terms I can) towards the Episcopal clergy dissenting from them, and deposed by them at the Revolution, is the charge I have always met with against them. . . .

The honest but prejudiced people in England, who have been imposed upon by the publick cryes of sufferings, persecutions, cruelties, and merciless usage of the Episcopal party in Scotland, will, I doubt not, be pleased to be undeceived, and be glad to restore the Church of Scotland to their entire charity and good opinion, and to have that damp removed, which they had on good ground, as they supposed, felt on their thoughts when they believed that the excesses pretended to had truth enough in them to merit real blame, and that the warmth of northern zeal had carryed the Scots beyond that moderation, which is the beauty and glory of the Protestant religion. . . .

I shall tell you that the Episcopal party in Scotland enjoy at this time, and have done for several years, all the liberty which the Dissenters in England do now enjoy, and that with conditions vastly differing:

1st They have their full liberty by the meer lenity and forbearance of the government, which in England could never be obtained but in little intervals but by act of parliament.

2. They have the same liberty, tho they not only refuse to take the oaths but refuse to sign the doctrinal Articles of the Confession of Faith, tho even the Church of England owns them to be all orthodox, a thing the Dissenters in England are not permitted in, no, not by Act of Tolleration.

3. They enjoy this liberty, notwithstanding they openly and in their publick assemblies not only omit praying for the Queen, but some of them actually and distinctly pray for their James the VIII and for his Restoration, which is not only praying for a popish prince, but praying God to depose or cut off her present Majesty, an affront so horridly impious, and so offensive to all her Majesties subjects, that one would wonder the most moderate principle in the world could bear with it.

And what will you say now gentlemen of the High Church in England, when I shall tell you, there are now fourteen or sixteen of these meeting-houses in the city of Edinburgh, just in the face of the General Assembly of the Church and in the eyes of the government, and that in any town or place in the kingdom where they have hearers, they have the same? That in some of these, they have newly set up the Common Prayer Book, a thing in the heighth of Episcopacy they never attempted, and which even the Episcopal party in general were never reconciled to? And that, in not one of these meetings that ever I heard of the Queen is pray'd for by name, but in some directly they pray for the King, which must mean their James the VIII, or worse, and in others they pray in ambiguous words, such as *The Queen*, or *The Royal Family*, and if I am not misinformed, in some for King James the Eighth in so many words.

'Tis true that in these open insults both of government and church they have in their turn met with some few oppositions from the people who have been provoked at such indignities done to their sovereign, and to the government in the face of the sun; and these little rabbles they would call persecution, and yet even in these cases the government has carefully supprest the tumult, and voluntarly made reparation to private families for the damnages they have pretended to have sustained, and that often beyond the real spoil, tho' at the same time their own imprudent and provoking carriage has been the principal occasion of these damnages; and this is evident in the city of Glasgow in particular, the only time they can talk of, where the rabble assaulting a Jacobite conventicle or Episcopal meeting, for there is very little difference between them at any time, and less there than on most occasions, the city payed the owner of the house several hundred pounds sterling for the supposed damnage he received; which in all appearance so far exceeded his loss that 'tis no breach of charity to believe he would be pleased to have his house rabbled once a week at the same price.

(*An Historical Account of the Bitter Sufferings and Melancholly Circumstances of the Episcopal Church in Scotland, under the Barbarous Usage and Bloody Persecution of the Presbyterian Church Government*, Edinburgh, August 1707)

THREATS TO MINISTERS OF THE CHURCH OF SCOTLAND

Defoe took much more seriously the attempt by Episcopalians to interfere with a Church of Scotland planting of a new minister in the parish of Gairloch in 1711, and went so far as to reprint in his *Review* the actual report from the Synod of Ross to the General Assembly detailing the harassment suffered by the presbytery representative sent to read the appropriate edict.

For the benefit of English readers, Defoe begins his article with an explanation of the usual procedure for introducing a new Presbyterian minister to his parish and the all too common obstruction encountered from Episcopalian landowners.

As the Presbyterian Church is thus establish'd, one part of their Establishment consists in a right or privilege of planting ministers in vacant churches, which right is understood in this manner. When a minister dies, the heretors, *Anglicé* lords of the mannor, together with the people, sign a call to such minister as they desire to succeed, which call is moderated, as they call it, that is, confirm'd by the presbytery of the bounds, and then the minister is admitted and, if he was not before, is ordain'd.

If the heretor refuses or delays to call a minister for a certain time, and after certain notices given as the law directs, the right of calling and planting a ministry lies *jure devoluto* in the presbytery of the bounds. . . .

Now in opposition to this known right, the heretors of these parishes, who are generally Episcopal, and almost as generally Jacobites, encourage, support and maintain Episcopal ministers, deposed and deprived by the law not to preach among them; only pray mark that, for that is not deny'd them, but to enter by force into the churches, possess the manse or parsonage house, and receive the stipend; and this is call'd *intrusion*, which by law is punish'd with banishment.

When the Presbyterian judicatories of the Church comes to judge in this case, they send ministers to those parishes and plant them there *jure devoluto*, as above, and in doing this they frequently meet with such treatment we have formerly related at Old Deer, and of which I shall now give more horrible examples. . . .

Here follows the report sent to the General Assembly from the Synod of Ross and Sutherland, in the case of Mr Chisholm, who was sent by the presbytery to read the edict or decree of the said presbytery, for planting Mr J. Morison in the vacant church of Gearloch.

At Cromartie, 12 April, 1711

Mr Thomas Chisholm, according to appointment of the presbytery, took journey towards Gearloch, about — day of February last, and that night lodged in the country of Strathwren [Strahern]; and that upon the morrow late at night he came to Kinlochow [Kinlochewe], a part of the parish of Gearloch belonging to Sir John MacKenzie of Coul, from which place he designed that night to go by boat to the other end of the loch. But the people of that place understanding his design stop'd all the boats, and shut all their houses. They would neither afford him lodging, nor allow him to cross the water towards the kirk, which oblig'd him to travel 5 miles in the night by the loch-side, and when he hired a boat in order to go off the next morning to that part of the country where the kirk lay. But that night about 2 in the morning, a party of armed men, about 16 in number, broke up the door of the house where he lodg'd, drag'd his 2 servants by the heels out of their beds naked out of the house, raised himself out of his bed, and compell'd him to return with them 10 Miles before daylight the same way from whence he came, and then left him on a hill several miles from any house without meat or drink; and when one of his servants fainted that night, his guard would not allow him (tho' he had come to the door of a house where they sold liquors) to take a dram thereof to refresh himself or revive his servant, but told him they did him but too great a complement when they suffer'd him to live. So that he was necessitate to leave his servant there and in that case, and himself with the other servant essay'd to return toward Gearloch another way, hiring a guide to lead him into Lochbroom, and from thence was resolv'd to go to Gearloch. But when he came within 3 miles of the country of Lochbroom, the hills there being so high, and the snow being so deep, and being fasting, watching and travelling the whole night before; and that day he fainted, where he lay speechless on the snow for an hour and an half. His guide seeing him in that condition, threatned to leave him, which he had done, had he not been forced by his servant to attend. After his reviving he travell'd several miles till he came late that night to the house of Ferhquare Mac Craw[27] in Lochbroom, where he lodg'd all that night. But after midnight a party of 8 or 9 men well arm'd broke into the house, and had taken him away instantly, had not his landlord interpos'd for a delay till day-light, which when it appear'd they compell'd him back again to Kinlochow, where after he comes notwithstanding all the fatigue he had met with that day, they would not allow him to go within a house, but kept guard on him in the open fields. In the mean time, a new company all in disguise reliev'd the former company, and brought him back again 3 miles to a wast-house[28] in a wood, where they kept him till 11 a clock the next day, being Saturnday, but before he left that place, being within the parish of Gearloch, he read the edict in the hearing of those who guarded him that night.

The men that guarded him thus did not understand what his reading was, but said one to another, "Doe not believe a word he says." Thus he did his business which he went for as effectually as if they had not medled with him; for a formal reading the edict within the paroch was all that the law requir'd.

That party being reliev'd by another party of 15 men, oblig'd him to travel that day thro' hills and waters till he came again within 4 miles of Lochbroom, where the company was divided and 7 of them convey'd him thro' many deep waters, some whereof reached very near his arm-pits. Upon the Saturnday late they brought him to the remotest bounds of the parish of Contein [Contin]. There they lodg'd with him all night. He proposed to some of the people of that country to preach to them, the next day being the sabbath, and the people shew'd their willingness to hear him. But he was no sooner up in the morning than they drag'd him away forward and told him that they were under command not to part with him till they brought him to Fouls [Foulis]; that when they came within sight of Contein they left him. One of them at their departure drawing him aside, said, he ought not to be angry at them for his treatment, feeling they did nothing but what they were commanded to do by Sir John MacKenzie of Coul, their master, whom they could not disobey; and likewise told him that it would be in vain for him, or any other Presbyterian minister, to attempt the going to Gearloch, for Sir John had guarded all passes to that country. Mr Chisholm that afternoon went forward to the ferry-town of Brahan[29] where he refreshed himself with some meat and drink about 7 of the clock in the afternoon upon the sabbath-day, being kept from eating any food by the several companies that guarded him from Friday's morning till then; and his legs and thighs were so cut with the snow and ice (being oblig'd to travel in a belted plaid) that for several days after he came home he was not in caise to rise out of his bed.

(*Review*, Tuesday, 21 May, 1711)

CRISIS

Within a year of Defoe's published account of the Gairloch episode, the Patronage Act restored the right of lay patrons to present ministers, Episcopal meetings were legally tolerated, and a bill was before parliament to set up the English liturgy in Scotland. Defoe believed that these developments encouraged the 'Episcopal and Jacobite party, for they are but one party' to sap 'the foundations of the Union'. Reminding the British Government of its obligation to protect the Church of Scotland from these attacks, he invokes again the marriage metaphor for the Union when he asserts that the wife (the Church of Scotland) deserves the protection of her spouse (the Government).

It was the peculiar of this Union, and what more especially pinch'd the Jacobite party in Scotland, that it settled the Presbyterian Church and the succession of Hanover; and as these were both incompatible with the interests of that party, either as Episcopal in principles or as Jacobite in politicks, they watch'd their opportunities on all occasions to supplant the one that the other might fall of course; and both these were to be done by a breach on the Union. . . . The Presbyterian Church is now under the general protection of the Parliament and the government; and it is a debt and the duty of the administration to defend the said Presbyterian establishment against the invasions of their own Jacobite and Episcopal disturbers. If a woman is single she may be insulted and made afraid by her own relations; she is liable to arrests, prosecutions, and all kinds of legal process for debts, trespass &c., but when she is married she is under covert, and her husband is her protector and defender. . . .

The designs of the Episcopal and Jacobite party, for they are but one party and one people in Scotland, having been manifestly driven on at the ruin of the Presbyterian establishment there, they knew it was impossible to bring this to pass, but by sapping the foundations of the Union, which had declar'd the said establishment of the church, as well as many other things, to be *unalterable*. This crabbed, unhappy word they could not bear, for if it remain'd they could never master the Presbyterian Settlement which was the eye-sore of the party, both there and here, and which the Union had perpetuated.

To this purpose they bent all their little cavils at this fatal word *unalterable*, which if they could but get over every thing would be easie to them after it; and as often as they can get a Jacobite ascendant in the ministry or Parliament they will push at that fundamental constitution of Britain, the Union. . . .

It seems a very unhappy crisis that a Treaty of Union being, with the greatest solemnity imaginable, made with the Scots, vast sums given to the Scots, and some spent in the bringing the great transaction to pass, it should within less than five year become a question among us, whither this Union can be broken by us, or no. It seem'd much more reasonable to expect that the publick should have study'd ways and means farther to confirm and establish the said Union, and to cultivate and improve it, letting the people of Scotland see that they were gainers, and should be improv'd by the Union; that they should taste of the sweets of English liberty, and that trade should flow in upon them, and their wealth and riches encrease.

But instead of this, the Jacobite and Episcopal party study'd all the ways they could devise to insult and affront the constitution of the Church, and finding all things ripe for their designs, they began in Parliament by getting a bill to be brought in for setting up the English liturgy in Scotland and tollerating the Episcopal meetings, &c.

(*The Present State of the Parties in Great Britain: particularly an enquiry into the state of Dissenters in England, and the Presbyterians in Scotland*, London, May 1712)

Raising the Old Devil: The Cameronians

Defoe's attitude to the Cameronians was much more lenient. He considered them to be misguided, and certainly not a serious threat to the established church or the government. In his *Review* he attacked the rival newspaper, *The Post-Boy*, for misrepresenting them.

Being thus as we are a nation of believers, you cannot wonder if I expect you should have a formal story handed to you from Scotland, about a great confluence of people meeting in the west and renewing the covenant, excommunicating sundry people and, among the rest, even the Parliament, the Presbyterian ministers, and the Queen herself. . . .

I cannot doubt, I say, but Mr *Post-Boy* from his constant correspondents in the north will have a long account to give you of this meeting of the Cameronians, and that this account shall be dress'd up in a form to please the believers on his side, *viz.* that at a field meeting (perhaps he may call it a rebellion, tho' by the way the poor people had no arms), a great number of people, 8 or 9000 in number, were assembled; that their meeting was for their religious worship, but that they cursed the Queen, the Parliament, &c., and much more, which the help of art may put in to illustrate this account.

Now that you may take every thing with you, I shall let you know in the general that the fact is true, and that the poor rash people have gone this length in their great field meeting for the sacrament. In short, the case is this, that as by the effect of a modern step of northern politicks we have raised an old devil, which good men thought had been almost laid a long time ago, and the raising this devil has been the aim and design of those people in Scotland who have push'd at dividing and inflaming the people, and they have, in part, brought it to pass. But since matters of this consequence ought to be set in a true light, and the false representations of the enemies of Scotland anticipated by a true account of things, for that reason I shall only prepare the world to hear the false account by first giving them a true state of the fact, and when this is done let them make their best of the story.

1. It is true that in the west of Scotland there are still remaining a few and, God be praised, by the Revolution and the endeavours of the establish'd Presbyterian ministers in Scotland they brought to a very few and those every day decreasing, of those people who were formerly call'd Cameronians, who always stood out from the Revolution Settlement, would never join with the Church, either in communion so much as hear their ministers, or submit to either the civil or ecclesiastick constitution. What the differences are, on what principles they act, and what the dispute is, these are things too long to enter on here, but I may give a particular of them hereafter. These people had but one leader, *viz.* Mr MacMellan, and have since an assistant, one Mr MacNeil; the one an ordain'd minister, but depos'd, the other not ordain'd, and neither of them of any character or capacity, other than is peculiar to the unhappy people themselves.

2. It is true and undeniable, even the Episcopal men in Scotland must own and acknowledge it, that the establish'd Church of Scotland, *viz.* the Presbyterians, reject, disown, and discountenance these people, and are rejected and disown'd by them; and that they have judicially, long ago, depos'd the said Mr Mac-Mellan from the office of a minister on the very account of these things; and this is prov'd past any reply: 1. On the kirk part by the records and judicial process against him, and by many Acts and Synods of Assembly against him and his followers; and 2dly, on their part, by their renouncing and excommunicating the ministers of the Church of Scotland in general, at the time of the general combination now spoken of.

3. It is yet as true as all this that the late imposition of oaths,

contrary to principle and, as I think (speaking my conscience and opinion only) expresly against the late Union, by which many scrupulous and dissatisfyed tho' good and conscientious people are driven to divide and separate from the establish'd Presbyterian Church in Scotland, has been a very great occasion of encreasing the numbers of these unhappy people, and consequently of all the disorders which may follow.

4. As to the extravagancies of these poor people, their excommunicating the Queen and the Parliament, and the ministers of the Church, as they are the effect of a misled judgment, and as there is nothing formidable in the power of numbers of the people, they seem to merit the compassion and pity of the government rather than their resentment; and it is hoped there may be other ways to reduce them than such bloody methods as were practised in the former times, since it has been found that lenity, forbearance and patience has lessened their numbers; whereas persecution, blood, hangman, and dragoons, always encreas'd them.

Let those then who are for calling fire from heaven upon these poor people, remember our Lord's admonition, *Ye know not what spirit ye are of*, and let them consider that every mistaken opinion is not immediately to be pursu'd with blood. Let them remove the cause, and take off the impositions and encroachments on the consciences of these poor people, and the thing will die of itself, the fire will go out, and the people will return of course to peace and duty. If there are any who delight in wicked purposes to animate this people, and blow up this fire into a national flame and confusion, that they may have an occasion thereby to overthrow and destroy the constitution of Scotland, let His glory, whose Face is a Flame of Fire, and who is King and Head of the Church, overthrow and destroy them. *Amen.*

(*Review*, Saturday, 30 August 1712) [30]

IGNORANCE OF CHRISTIANITY IN THE HIGHLANDS

Finally, in marked contrast to Jacobite-sympathetic Episcopalians in the north-east and extremist Covenanters of various hues in the south-west, Defoe found, to his great surprise, on touring the Scottish Highlands, a high level of ignorance of Christianity. He was optimistic, however, that George I's provision of £1,000 per annum to the General Assembly for sending missionaries into the areas would ensure a happy result.

Should we go about here to give you an account of the religion of the people in this country, it would be an unpleasant work, and perhaps scarce seem to deserve credit. You would hardly believe that in a Christian island, as this is said to be, there should be people found who know so little of religion, or of the custom of Christians, as not to know a Sunday or sabbath from a working day, or the worship of God from an ordinary meeting for conversation. I do not affirm that it is so, and I shall say no more of it here because I would not publish it, for it is to be hoped [it] may in time find redress; but I cannot but say that his Majesty's gift of 1000 l. annually to the Assembly of Scotland for sending ministers or missionaries for the propagating Christian knowledge in the Highlands is certainly one of the most needful charities that could have been thought of, worthy of a king, and well suited to that occasion; and if prudently applyed, as there is reason to believe it will be, may in time break in upon this horrible ignorance, that has so far spread over this unhappy part of the country.

On the other hand, what shall we say to the neglect which for so many years past has been the occasion of this surprizing darkness among the people, when the poor abandoned creatures have not so much as had the common instruction of Christianity, so much as to know whether there was any such thing as a God or no, much less how to worship him? And if at any time any glympse of light had been infussed into them, and they had been taught any knowledge of superior things, it has been by the diligence of the popish clergy who, to do them justice, have shewn more charity and taken more pains that way than some whose work it had been, and who it might much more have been expected from?

(*A Tour of the Whole Island of Great Britain, 1724-6*)

Map of Scotland that appeared in the first and some later editions of Defoe's *A Tour through the Whole Island of Great Britain*. It was probably drawn by Defoe's friend, Herman Moll

CHAPTER 5

Scots and Scotland

Supposing Scots men to be no monsters,
but made of flesh and blood like other people
– Review, 12 July, 1709 –

If Defoe regretted the ignorance of Christianity in the Highlands of Scotland, he certainly deplored the abysmal ignorance of Scotland in England. He was better informed than most of his countrymen, largely as a result of the time he spent north of the border, working in the capital and taking what opportunities he could to travel around the Scottish kingdom. As he wrote in his Account and Description of Scotland in his *Tour*, 'the world shall, for once, hear what account an Englishman shall give of Scotland, who has had occasion to see most of it'. Notably, he says, 'I shall not make a Paradise of Scotland . . . I shall endeavour to show what it really is.'

As well as enlightening the English about the real Scotland, during the years he promoted the Union and warned of the dangers of Jacobitism in pamphlets and the *Review*, he cast himself as Scotland's advocate, especially to the Scots, and did his best to persuade both nations to overcome their longstanding prejudices and ancient resentments. He tried to set the record straight on a number of historical events, some quite recent like the Massacre of Glencoe, that fed these hostilities, and often used metaphors to encourage closer and better relations: the two kingdoms are not only neighbours, but siblings or twins, or spouses, with Scotland too often finding herself the wronged 'wife'.

MISCONCEPTIONS

In all his writing about Scotland and Scottish affairs, Defoe's perspective is fundamentally anglocentric. He never forgot that he was an outsider, a 'stranger' as he often described himself, and although he occasionally expressed fears for his life – hardly groundless given his activities as an English spy in Scotland – he also paid tribute to Scottish hospitality and courtesy towards strangers. These are qualities he highlights in a *Review* article whose main thrust is the serious misconceptions that exist even among educated English people.

To hear our people speak of Scotland, or of the Scots affairs or people, it would make a stranger think that this same place call'd Scotland was some remote country in the East-Indies, or about Madagascar, or some island in the Fretum Magellanicum, the North West passages, the South Seas, or somewhere very unfrequented, where very few people ever came, and from whence, like our news from Muscovy, things were very uncertainly related and our accounts from thence very little to be depended upon.

The learned gentlemen of this party, tho' skill'd in history, masters of geography, and have seen [a] great part of the world in their travels, they'll tell you that Scotland is a barren, uncultivated, desolate country; that the land is all barren, and will hardly maintain the people that live there. Nay, they will very learnedly ask sometimes if there is any mutton, or any beef, or any butter, or any such thing as milk in Scotland. The Highlanders they take to be a sort of monsters, and ask if they live upon roots and the bark of the trees. Never was more wild notions in the heads of our people here of the Carribees in the Gulph of Florida, and the Islands of the Gulph of Mexico, or of the brutish people of the Cape de Bonne Esperance, than they have of this people. Nay, one but the other day, who is a man of letters and a man of history, seriously and for real information ask'd me what sort of speech the Scots tongue was, for that he had never met with any books of it. Another ask'd me as seriously, being a merchant, where the Scots fetch'd their corn before the Union and what they had to buy it with.

I could add a great many such as these, as the constant result of the most profound and mysterial ignorance that ever was yet found among a knowing people, such as we pretend to be. From all which I see a great deal of room to confirm the first maxim I laid down to myself when I had begun to enquire of, and consider Scotland, its people and circumstances, *viz.* that there are not in the whole world two nations, that stand so near, have so much concern with and interest in each other, that know so little of one another, as these two. . . .

Gentlemen, if the Scots want money, I must tell you, they do not want manners; and one piece of humanity they are masters of, which you with all your boasted improvements are without, and that is, courtesie to strangers, in which they out-do even the French themselves. But this by the way. . . .

Scotland really is so far from starving her inhabitants from any real defect of the land that it cannot really be call'd a barren soil. The defect of Scotland is from the want of application of the land; by management and right cultivation, enclosing and improving, not for want of the land making a suitable return of profit and advantage to the industrious husband-man, when he has done. . . .

There are in Scotland, and that 150 miles north of Edinburgh as well as nearer to Edinburgh, whole counties, vast tracks of land for 20 miles together, as rich, as strong, as fertile, as well water'd, and as capable of improvement, as the counties of Middlesex, Hartford, and Bedford, or generally speaking, as any in England.

But Scotland has been an uninstructed, discourag'd and abus'd nation; poverty has grown upon them. Misery begets sloth, according to an old English proverb, that bare walls make giddy housewives; and sloth confirms and binds down that misery. The disasters of war, English devastations, the disasters of their government, their courts being remov'd to England, and above all, the disasters of their constitution, the want of that thing call'd liberty, and the petty tyranny of the landlords, these have all kept Scotland poor. But take this if you please from me: rouze but the Scots to industry by such encouragements as you both may and ought to give them, they have a soil able to make them as rich, as plentiful, and as pleasant as your selves.

(*Review*, Thursday, 14 July 1709)

Dog's Abuse

England's neglect of Scotland is likened to marital abuse in another article, written as talk about breaking the Union became common and the Jacobite threat became more alarming towards the end of Queen Anne's reign.

I cannot let you part without giving you one word in behalf of poor Scotland, a nation to the highest degree, at least as I think, maltreated, nay, unkindly and unfriendly treated by you all. I can compare it to nothing so well as to a bad husband, who had been the most passionate woer imaginable, but uses his wife like a dog as soon as he is married. When the Union was making, all the encouragement in the world was given to the Scots to expect good treatment at our hands, and her Majesty, who does not willingly, I dare say, see the present distress of the people, gave us all encouragement to use them well.

(*Review*, Saturday, 15 November 1712)

ADDRESSING THE PROBLEM

He even issued Edinburgh editions of his *Review* from 1709 in a bid to curry favour with the Scots. In the introduction to the first issue Defoe, 'the Author', assures his readers in 'North Britain' of his commitment to both 'the service of Scotland' and impartial reportage. In addition, through a combination of fairly unsubtle ingratiation and self-promotion, he presents himself as a mediator between the disputing parties.

If he thought you would not mistake him and say he is flattering you, a thing he abhors, he would say he finds reason to hope for better treatment here than he has found elsewhere, having, generally speaking, seen a greater propensity to right information and impartial judging here than in other places. Again, he hopes to plead some merit among you, gentlemen of North Britain, *viz.* that this paper has been for some time, and will always be while this author lives, calculated for the service of Scotland, to defend her against reproach, set her right in the judgments and opinions of her neighbours, and set them right in their judgments and opinions concerning her; to represent Scotland right in England, and represent things in England right to Scotland. And if this be impartially pursued, the author hopes for a better reception than in other cases he complains of; . . . it shall, on all occasions, be peculiarly pointed to the advantage of Scotland in her religious, civil, trading and improving capacities.

(*Review*, Edinburgh, Thursday, 31 March 1709)

HISTORICAL GRIEVANCES

BANNOCKBURN

As part of his effort to reconcile Scots and English, Defoe also reminded them of their bloody, war-dominated history and encouraged them to put aside grievances associated with long past and more recent 'massacres' like Bannockburn and Glencoe.

Whether the Scots magnify this victory or not, is not my business. That it was a total overthrow of the English army is certain, and that abundance of the English nobility and gentry lost their lives there; but 'tis as true that it was the ill conduct of the English at that time and the unfortunate king that led them on which were the occasion. His glorious predecessor, Edward I, or Edward III, his more glorious successor, never lost such a battle. But let the fault be where it will, this is certain: that the English lost the day, and were horribly massacred by the Scots, as well after as in the fight, for the animosity was implacable between the two nations, and they gave but little quarter on either side.

(*A Tour through the Whole Island of Great Britain, 1724–6*)

MASSACRE OF GLENCOE

Most of his heroes were contemporaries, and included King William III, whose praises he sang during and after his lifetime, and whose honour he defends in relation to the Glencoe massacre. While he does not deny that the MacDonald clan was treated barbarously, Defoe's main purpose is to exonerate the king.

The affair of Glenco was another step to national breaches. . . . That the Glenco men among several other clans of the Highlanders were enemies to the government at that time, had been in arms under Dundee, and had on all occasions shown their implacable aversion to King William and all the interest of the Revolution needs no proof, and is own'd even by the greatest friends to the cause.

That these people were not only very troublesome, but dangerous, and had committed several hostilities, murders, robberies and depredations, on both the innocent country people their neighbours, as well as on the garrisons of souldiers plac'd on that side to suppress them, is also out of dispute.

The defence made for this is short: that they were fair enemies and had profess't open war.

As his Majesty had this account given him of these people, and I do not find but it was a true account too, it was the advice of the general and officers imployed at that time that it was a mischief which as times then went might be very dangerous to the publick, & that therefore it behoved them to take some immediate course with them. And since desperate mischiefs require remedies of the same kind, they thought the first force the best and proposed to march immediately with a body of troops into the place, and intirely root them out as a den of thieves and destroyers, without which the peaceable subjects could never be safe, nor the government be easie. That the charge of maintaining troops there was an intolerable burden to the countrey, and as there was no other way could prevail to preserve the peace, it was absolutely necessary to come to extremity.

His Majesty, who by his experience in military affairs was soon convinc'd both of the justice in point of war & necessity in point of government of this advice, yet out of his meer goodness of disposition & general clemency, answered, he agreed to their reasons, but required that before any such extremities should be used with them, a proclamation should be published offering pardon or remission for all violences and villanies past to all these people without exception who, within a certain time should come in, lay down their arms, and submit to the government, and take the oaths as peaceable subjects.

'Tis here visible that his Majesties intentions were not only just and honourable to these people, tho his implacable enemies, but that he resolved like a merciful prince, to try all reasonable methods of tenderness and goodness, if possible, to keep the peace and save the offenders too.

With this proclamation, commission was given to the military power if this merciful method could not prevail, they should proceed to extremities, and by force of arms destroy all those that should stand out and not comply with the proclamation.

It is certain, and all men allow, that the Glenco-men had not complyed with the proclamation; nay they had rejected two indemnities.

I know 'tis objected that Glenco came and took the oath six days after the time, made a legal and just excuse, and sent word of his willingness to comply with it, and that it was only a trespass of time, which they supposed he had repaired, that the end of the proclamation was answered and that the king who was mercifully inclin'd would never have taken the lives of people resolved to submit for a trespass of days.

To this I answer, as his Majesty himself did in that case, that indeed had he been in the field, and on the spot, and that excuse had been sent to him, he might have accepted it, but that as commissions in cases of war are to be punctually executed, he could not require it of the officers to accept it as an excuse against a positive proclamation and an express order. Besides, I do not find any but the chief had gone thus far, the rest not having come in at all.

It is alledged that the execution was from private malice; but none could ever yet have the face to charge his Majesty with that, and I could never hear of any reason given why the commanders of the forces should have any, much less those at whom the scandal of it was pointed, upon pretence of giving unwarrantable orders.

But the case chiefly lyes here: the men fell under the misfortune of a crisis in war, they brought themeselves into it by an omission of time; to say, they could not avoid it, does not reach the case. If the officers can be charged with any private revenge in this case, I have only this to say:

1. I never yet saw any reason to think so. No personal grudge or quarrel ever appeared, that I ever met with, or was so much as alledged in it, or gain pretended to be made by it. If the E. of B[readalbane] had any private game, it neither affected the king, nor the other persons charged with the thing.

2. If it were so, it no way affects the king, against whom the reproach of this affair is since pointed, who acted nothing but what was agreeable to the laws of war, and mixt it with that general blessing of his temper, an unusual clemency.

If the commission given was executed with barbarity and blood, killing people in what we call cold blood, surprizing them in peace and dependence on safety, all this will turn upon the merits of the first cause; for if they were by the laws of war to be destroyed, all manner of surprizes become justified by the same law. As to the cruelties and excesses of the furious soldiers, no man can have the face to reproach his Majesty with that.

The grand question remains yet behind, why did not the king cause the offenders to be made examples, and severely punish the murderers? I shall answer:

1. If his Majesties peculiar[31] was too much clemency, I think some of those that make loudest exclamations on this article ought to be silent since, had exemplar justice been his Majesties employment from his first landing, we should have no reason to have said it was a bloodless revolution, nor they perhaps have been alive to complain.

2. For the reasons aforesaid, his Majesty often said it was a moot-point in war whether they had broke orders or no, and tho' I have the honour to know that his Majesty exceedingly resented the manner, yet it did not appear at all that they had laid themselves open to miltary justice in it, or so much as given ground to call them to account before a council of war.

As to national or civil justice, the memory of the king can never be reflected upon in that, unless some persons had pursued them at law, obtained sentence against them, and his Majesty had protected them from the prosecution or execution of such sentences.

Thus far, I think, the king himself is intirely clear of this matter. Who else may have been guilty, and how, either of breaking orders, going beyond them on niceties, and executing them with barbarities, I have no occasion to enter upon here. I shall be far from defending such things, and I am sure his Majesty was far from approving it.

It might be said here, you have no occasion to defend the king's memory in this case, since the Parliament of Scotland clear'd his Majesty by their unanimous vote of 14th. of June, *viz.* that his Majesties instructions contained no warrant for the execution of the Glenco men.

I shall only note that it is true the Parliament past such a vote, and 'tis as true the king resented very ill their usage of him, as he had great reason to do, frequently repeating, that he thanked the Parliament of Scotland – they had used him better than England had done his grandfather, for they had tryed him for his life and brought him in "NOT GUILTY". I must confess, it was very unaccountable the House should pass such a vote upon their sovereign, whom no man had had the impudence to owne a reflection.

(*History of the Union*, Edinburgh, 1709)

THE SCOTS

Given the frequent and often lengthy periods of time Defoe spent in Scotland, he got to know some of the inhabitants well. What he observed at close hand of many of the major players on the political scene is captured in character sketches, most of which he published. Something of the foreignness of Scots to an English incomer is also conveyed in his writing, including his fiction. In his novel *Colonel Jack* he describes what strikes an English thief on the run from the law, and his companion the narrator, when they first encounter both impoverished Scots in the countryside and wealthy gentlemen among the crowds at Edinburgh's Mercat Cross. Of course, Defoe himself had some experience of seeking cover in a strange land and of being intimidated by 'ill-natured' Scots.

I asked him then how he intended to manage himself in that country? He said in a few words, he did not know yet, he doubted the people were very poor; but if they had any money he was resolved to have some of it.

[W]e . . . went on towards the capital city. On the road we found too much poverty, and too few people, to give him room to expect any advantage in his way; and though he had his eyes about him as sharp as a hawk, yet he saw plainly there was nothing to be done; for as to the men, they did not seem to have much money about them; and for the women, their dress was such, that had they any money, or indeed any pockets, it was impossible to come at them; for, wearing large plaids about them and down to their knees, they were wrapped up so close, that there was no coming to make the least attempt of that kind.

We . . . went forward to Edinburgh. All the way thither we went through no considerable town, and it was but very coarse travelling for us, who were strangers; for we met with waters which were very dangerous to pass, by reason of hasty rains, at a place called Lauderdale . . . the next day after we came thither; my captain having a desire to walk, and look about him, asked me if I would go and see the town? I told him yes; so we went out, and coming through a gate, that they call the Nether-bow, into the great High-street, which went up to the cross, we were surprised to see it thronged with an infinite number of people. Ay (says my captain), this will do; however, as I had made him promise to make no adventures that day, otherwise I told him I would not go out with him, so I held him by the sleeve, and would not let him stir from me.

Then we came up to the market-cross, and there, besides the great number of people who passed and repassed, we saw a great parade, or kind of meeting, like an exchange of gentlemen, of all ranks and qualities, and this encouraged my captain again, and he pleased himself with that sight.

It was while we were looking, and wondering at what we saw here, that we were surprised with a sight which we little expected; we observed the people running on a sudden, as to see some strange thing just coming along, and strange it was indeed; for we saw two men naked from the waist upwards, run by us as swift as the wind, and we imagined nothing but that it was two men running a race for some mighty wager. On a sudden we found two long small ropes or lines, which hung down at first, pulled straight, and the two racers stopped, and stood still, one close by the other. We could not imagine what this meant, but the reader may judge at our surprise, when we found a man follow after, who had the ends of both those lines in his hands, and who, when he came up to them, gave each of them two frightful lashes with a wire whip, or lash, which he held in the other hand; and then the two poor naked wretches run on again to the length of their line or tether, where they waited for the like salutation; and in this manner they danced the length of the whole street, which is about half a mile.

This was a dark prospect to my captain, and put him in mind, not only of what he was to expect if he made a slip in the way of his profession in this place, but also of what he had suffered, when he was but a boy, at the famous place called Bridewell.

But this was not all; for, as we saw the execution, so we were curious to examine into the crime too; and we asked a young fellow who stood near us, what the two men had done, for which they suffered that punishment? The fellow, an unhappy ill-natured Scotchman, perceived by our speech that we were Englishmen, and by our question that we were strangers, told us, with a malicious wit, that they were two Englishmen; and that they were whipped so for picking pockets, and other petty thieveries, and that they were afterwards to be sent away over the border into England.

Now this was every word of it false, and was only formed by his nimble invention to insult us as Englishmen; for when we inquired farther, they were both Scotchmen, and were thus scourged for the usual offences, for which we give the like punishment in England; and the man who held the line and scourged them, was the city hangman; who (by the way) is there an officer of note, has a constant salary, and is a man of substance; and not only so, but a most dexterous fellow in his office, and makes a great deal of money of his employment.[32]

(From *Colonel Jack*, 1723)

On Highlanders

In a long digression on Highlanders within his tract on the 1715 Jacobite Rebellion, Defoe aims to allay English fears about these legendary 'wild men', by describing their dress, customs and the clan system.

The Highlander garters his stockings below the knees and wears no breeches in the coldest season, but his plaid which is belted about him, and his trouze hanging from his wast to the middle of the thigh and something lower serves him instead of breeches, and hangs loose to his thigh, open below, but plaited and full like the vallens of a bed, and not unlike the skirts of the old Roman habit, which always hung loose upon the thigh.

By this dress his knee is naked for about two hands length above and below, and the hamstrings being thus free from the garters, they suppose themselves more nimble and easy; nor is the cold which their other parts are hereby exposed to any grievance to them, but they bear it as readily as we do in our faces or hands, or other parts daily exposed, which makes them very hardy.

They have besides this their plaid, a loose garment in the nature of a robe, which they carry as it were on their arm. It is thrown over their shoulder, and tho' to our imagination it seems to be very cumbersome, yet as they never go without it, they are so dexterous in the casting it about them and handling it, that it is no hindrance to them at all, either in their running or handling their weapons; on the contrary, they make it very serviceable in their fighting, by covering one half of their body with it, especially their left arm and shoulders, in such a manner as no sword can cut thro' it, but that which it is more particularly serviceable to them for is, that they lodge in it as in a house, or that they may be said to carry their tents always about them; and when they come into the field, they shall lodge more warm, wrapt up in their plaid, than they think the other soldiers can do in their tents. . . .

Gentlemen will be gentlemen in all nations of the world, but these wild Highlandmen may well be stiled wild men, for they act the brutal part to perfection, being voratious, cruel, insolent and unmerciful in their prosperity, and basely servile or sullen if they are subdued.

(From *A View of the Scots Rebellion*, 1715)

FAMOUS AND INFAMOUS SCOTS

Individual Scots, famous and infamous on both sides of the border, claimed his attention too, and he left short character sketches of a number of these. The Scottish peers who played a significant role in facilitating the Union, the Duke of Queensberry and the Marquis (later Duke) of Montrose, both of whom patronised Defoe, receive his special commendation, while the Duke of Argyll, Queensberry's successor as High Commissioner, incurs his disapproval, largely because of his excesses, and perhaps not a little on account of his orchestration of the 1710 'election' of peers to the British Parliament. Baron Belhaven, whose emotional anti-Union speech during the Scottish parliamentary debate on the treaty articles was mercilessly satirised by Defoe in 'The Vision: A Poem' (1706), nonetheless receives a very respectful obituary in his *Review*. Given Defoe's views on Jacobites, it comes as no surprise to learn he has nothing positive to say of the Old Pretender, and is inclined to belittle him as a 'vain scarecrow'. On the other hand, he seems to have had a sneaking respect for Rob Roy, notorious cattle thief and sometime Jacobite, if *The Highland Rogue*, published in 1723, is indeed by him. Of course, MacGregor's raids and evasions of capture were sensational even then as regular reports on his notorious activities appeared in newspapers and newssheets at the time. William Paterson may have helped Defoe obtain release from prison in 1704, but less than two years later Defoe clearly does not trust him. Concluding this section is a brief character of John White, the Edinburgh hangman, who might never have been known to posterity, had Defoe not memorialised him as a compassionate executioner.

WILLIAM WALLACE

In pursuing this article of a national peace between the two kingdoms, methinks nothing should more illustrate it to our thoughts than the memories of the animosities that have been between the two nations – with what inveteracy and unusual cruelty carried on! with what mutual barbarisms, cruel and unjust executions, as in case of brave Wallis!

(*Review*, Tuesday, 29 October 1706)

JAMES FRANCIS STUART, THE OLD PRETENDER

Why should not the good people of Britain be made easie, and their fears be turned into peaceable satisfaction, by seeing that this Devil may not be so black as he is painted; and that the noise made of the Pretender and the frightful things said of his coming and of his being receiv'd here, may not be made greater scarecrows to us than they really are.

(from *What if the Pretender Should Come?* London, 1713)

ROB ROY

Robert Mac-gregor, alias Rob-Roy, is the son of Calm Mac-gregor, second son to the laird of Mac-gregor, the chief of that name. He is a man of a prodigious strength, and of such an uncommon stature that he approaches even to a gigantic size. He wears a beard above a foot long, and not only his face, but his whole body, is cover'd over with red hair, which is the reason that he is commonly called Rob-Roy; for that (in the Highland dialect) signifies Red Robert, it being usual there to give people nick names from their hair or complexion. His habit is after the usual manner of Highlanders, who are perfect strangers to the English fashion of wearing breeches and stockings. . . .

He never wanted good intelligence, for he continually kept spies abroad; insomuch, that if any person came to visit a friend within ten or twelve miles of Craigroystone[33] he was assuredly catch'd by some of the Mac-gregors, convey'd away, and detain'd till the sum demanded was paid, which was seldom very long; for they were generally treated in such a manner as made them very importunate with their friends to dispatch the price of their redemption. But Rob-Roy did not always act with this severity, for sometimes if his prisoners appeared to be persons of credit, he'd grant them their freedom upon their promise of sending him the sum requir'd.

He gave a particular instance of his generosity to a gentleman whom he took one night from a friend's house. He kept him prisoner for several days in expectation of making some advantage by him; but finding that he had really been very much reduced by great losses, he not only set him at liberty, but supplied him with money to defray his travelling charges, and sent him in one of his own boats, with servants to attend him, as far as he could go by water.

But Captain Mac-gregor being now grown notorious, both for his robberies and rebellion, a proclamation was publish'd offering a reward of a thousand pounds to any person that should apprehend and bring him to justice.

Hereupon a certain great man in the north of Scotland[34] sent several messages to him, assuring him that if he would come in private to his house and satisfy him in some material points relating to the Rebellion,[35] his trouble should meet with no less a recompence than His Majesty's free pardon and favour, both to himself and his followers.

At length, by repeated intreaties and additional promises of protection and that, upon honour if he disliked the terms, he should have full liberty to return in safety, he was brought into a compliance to run the hazard.

By the King,

A PROCLAMATION

For the Difcovering and Apprehending *Robert Campbel* alias *Mac-Gregor*, commonly called *Rob Roy*, for the feveral Crimes therein mentioned.

GEORGE R.

WHEREAS We have received Information, That upon the Eight and Twentieth Day of *January* laft, a Party, confifting of an Officer and Twenty Men, marched in order to join another Party of the Tenants of the Duke of *Montrofe*, that were following a Parcel of Cattle, that had been ftolen from one *Drunlie*, a Tenant to the faid Duke of *Montrofe*; but it growing very dark the faid Party were obliged to take Quarters at *Glansfaloch*, in that Part of our united Kingdom of *Great Britain* called *Scotland*, where they were informed, that *Robert Campbel* alias *MacGregor*, commonly called *Rob Roy*, was .... gone from thence with a ftrong Party, confifting of near Fifty Men well armed, ... the faid Officer ...... Thefe Scotish upon the Whift as foon as he came there, not being ...... to go further that Night, and that they had not been there above Half an Hour before they heard feveral Shots; Upon which they were out and found one of the Sentinels ...., That the faid *Rob Roy's* Party fired feveral Times into the Houfe; but finding that to no Purpofe, they followed the Party that belonged to the Duke of *Montrofe*, and difarmed them all; and that the faid *Rob Roy* fhot one of the Men as he lay in his Bed: We, out of our Royal Inclination to Juftice, and to the Intent that the faid *Robert Campbel*, alias *MacGregor*, commonly called *Rob Roy*, may be apprehended and punifhed for his faid Offences, in Contempt of Our Royal Authority, and to the Deftruction of the Lives of Our Subjects, whereby all others may be deter'd from committing the like Crimes, have thought fit, by the Advice of Our Privy Council, to iffue this Our Royal Proclamation: And We are hereby gracioufly pleafed to promife, That if any Perfon fhall difcover the faid *Robert Campbel* alias *MacGregor*, commonly called *Rob Roy*, fo as he be apprehended and brought to Juftice for his faid Offences, fuch Difcoverer fhall have and receive, as a Reward for fuch Difcovery, the Sum of Two Hundred Pounds *Sterling*: Whereof our Commiffioners for executing the Office of Treafurer of Our Exchequer, are hereby required to make Payment accordingly; and if any Perfon who is a Rebel or an Accomplice with the faid *Rob Roy*, fhall make fuch Difcovery, as aforefaid, fuch Difcoverer fhall have and receive the faid Reward of Two Hundred Pounds *Sterling*, and alfo Our Gracious Pardon for his faid Offences. And We do hereby ftrictly Charge and Command all Our Juftices of the Peace, and all other Our Officers, and all other Our loving Subjects, that they do ufe their utmoft Diligence in their feveral Places and Capacities, to find out, difcover and apprehend the faid Offender in Order to his being brought to Juftice. And We do hereby Command that this Our Proclamation be publifhed in the ufual Form, that none may pretend Ignorance; And We ordain thefe Prefents to be printed, and Our Solicitor to difpatch Copies in the ufual Manner.

Given at Our Court at St. James's the 19th Day of March 1719, in the 5th Year of Our Reign.

GOD fave the King.

Printed by JAMES WATSON, One of His Majefty's Printers, 1719.

Royal Proclamation for the discovery and apprehension of Robert Campbell, alias MacGregor, also known as Rob Roy, National Archives of Scotland (SC/54/15/1)

The nobleman was walking in his garden when a servant brought him word that Mr Mac-gregor was arriv'd; upon which he gave orders to conduct him in.

At Rob-Roy's appearance the Duke, with a seeming fondness, ran to embrace him, protesting he knew not how to express the joy he felt at the sight of so brave a gentleman.

The compliments on both sides being over, his Grace began to be very inquisitive about persons concern'd in the late insurrection, and other things which Mac-gregor was unwilling to answer directly to.

The Duke told him that, if he expected to obtain a pardon, he must make a full and particular discovery. "If your Grace," says he, "had let me know as much by your messengers, it had sav'd me the labour of coming so far." "I never intended," says the Duke, "to give you this trouble to no purpose: for tho' at present you are not in a humor to satisfy my curiosity, 'tis possible your mind may alter in a few days, and therefore it may not be improper to detain you." "And am I then betray'd!" says Mac-gregor. "Has a man of your quality such a mercenary soul as to forfeit his word, his faith, his honour, and all for a pitiful reward?"

"Peace! Peace!" quoth the Duke and, stepping back, knockt at the garden-door, which being immediately open'd, a body of guards rush'd in.

Rob-Roy, in a most violent rage, laid his hands on his dagger with an intent to stab the Duke for his perfidy. But, instantly recollecting his reason, he consider'd such a rash action might prove of fatal consequence to himself, and that dissimulation might effect what would be impracticable by violence. He therefore quietly suffer'd 'em to carry him to prison.

Being there, (at Rob-Roy's earnest intreaty) the Duke coming to him, he, in a most submissive manner, beg'd his Grace's pardon; and promis'd him, if next day he might have liberty, he'd acquaint him not only with the particulars then desir'd, but with other affairs also much more material.

This so pleas'd the Duke that he was resolv'd to use all the fair means possible to engage him to perform his promise, and therefore order'd his guards to treat him with all the respect that was consistent with the safety of a prisoner. His Grace was so elate with the success of this enterprise that he forthwith dispatcht an express to the Lord Justice Clerk, who then resided at Edinburgh.

Upon which information, his Lordship immediately order'd a party of dragoons, then quartering at Linlithgow, to march to his Grace's seat and conduct Mr Mac-gregor to Edinburgh-goal; but, notwithstanding their expedition, they happen'd to arrive too late, as we shall find hereafter.

The Duke was not satisfy'd with transmitting this affair to his Lordship only; but, as if he thought fame was too idle in spreading the news of his management, he wrote another letter on the same subject to the Secretary of State at London and several more to other gentlemen, his friends and acquaintance; so that, in three or four days, there was scarce an inhabitant in North-Britain that had not receiv'd the welcome report of Mac-gregor's imprisonment.

Rob-Roy, in the mean time, was employing his thoughts about forming a scheme to regain his liberty; and, having resolv'd upon one that carry'd an air of success, it was presently put in execution.

He gain'd the hearts of his guard by frequently calling for large quantities of brandy, and other strong liquors, of which he had been accustom'd to drink so heartily that not a little would disorder him. The glass was handed about a-pace, the soldiers drank freely, and so did Rob-Roy himself to their thinking; but he generally deceiv'd 'em, by letting the liquor run thro' his beard which, the reader may remember, was of an extraordinary length. He was so far from appearing discontented at his present circumstances, that he was almost continually diverting the company with comical old songs and pleasant stories of his own adventures. . . .

When morning appear'd, Rob-Roy told his guards that he had a favour to beg of them. They were eager to know what it was, and swore (as intelligibly as the fumes of the brandy would let them) that they should think themselves the most ungrateful dogs in nature, if they deny'd any thing that was reasonable to a gentleman that had shew'd himself so generous. He thank'd 'em for their civility and added that he had reason to believe his great strength and the preservation of his health were chiefly owing to a constant practice of bathing himself every morning, and therefore hop'd that they would not deny him the liberty of continuing a custom which he had been us'd to from his infancy; and especially since the omission of it might be of ill consequence to him. They, without the least scruple, comply'd with his request, and readily attended him to a river that ran along by the side of the wood, in which he had given orders for a horse to be ready. He plung'd into the water and, bathing himself as usual, came out, seeing no sign of the horse, and return'd with his guard to the prison.

They were no sooner got in, but, as a gratuity for the favour they had granted him, he gives orders for a bowl of punch; which, being brought before 'em, they welcom'd it with loud acclamations of joy, and the cup ran merrily round, with "a health to the Duke and Captain Mac-gregor." But, in the height of their carousing, Rob-Roy puts his hand in his pocket and, in a seeming consternation, tells them he had lost his pocket-book since he went out last; that there were notes in it of great value besides some particular memorandums that nearly concern'd the Duke. They (as drunk as they were) express'd a great concern for his loss and unanimously offer'd their service to go with him and look for it. He thank'd them and, accepting their kindness, led them toward the river where, while they were diligently searching the grass, he suddenly call'd to them and bid them give over. They look'd up and were surpriz'd to see him well mounted. "My humble service to the Duke, your master," says he, "and pray assure his Grace, that I shall take all opportunities of returning the favours he has oblig'd me with." He spoke, and setting spurs to his horse, they were left in the utmost confusion, cursing one another, and damning the blood of the pocket-book. The news of this escape was quickly carried to the Duke, who order'd the poor intoxicated sinners to be taken into custody and severely punish'd for their negligence. The dragoons that arriv'd soon after with orders to convey the late prisoner to Edinburgh were oblig'd to return without him, and his Grace's conduct in the affair was, for a considerable time after, the common subject of lampoon.

(From *The Highland Rogue*, London, 1723)

DUKE OF QUEENSBERRY

This . . . Duke would require a history rather than a bare mention in a work of this kind. But I have forbid myself entring far into the character of persons and families and therefore, tho' I think myself bound to honour the merit of so great a person, I shall sum it all up in this: that as I had the honour to be known to his Grace, so I had the opportunity to see and read by his permission several letters written to him by the late King William with his own hand, and several more by Queen Anne, written also by her Majesty's own hand, with such expressions of their satisfaction in his fidelity and affection to their Majesties service, his ability and extraordinary judgement in the affairs entrusted to him, his knowledge of, and zeal for, the true interest of his country, and their dependence upon his councils and conduct, that no minister of state in Europe could desire greater testimonies of his services or a better character from his sovereign and this from different princes, and at the distance of several years from one another and, to be sure, without any manner of corresponding one with the other.

That this noble person was Lord Commissioner at the time of the Union, sat in the throne at the last Parliament of Scotland and touched with the sceptre the Act of Parliament which put an end to parliaments for ever in that part of Great Britain, will always be matter of history to the end of time. Whether the Scots will remember it to the advantage of the Duke's character in their opinion, that must be as their several opinions guide them.

(A Tour through the Whole Island of Great Britain)

DUKE OF ARGYLL

This was a young nobleman of great hopes, and from whom great things were expected on account of the very race he was descended from. Had he inherited the principles of his family as he did the honour and estate, he must have been the head of that very party he now acted against, being the same for whose cause two of his greatest ancestors at least had both ventur'd and lost their lives; but grace not going by generation, nor vertue by inheritance any more in that country than in ours, he neither own'd their cause or imitated their vertue, but gave himself up first to all manner of vice, and then with his morals abandon'd his principles flew in the face of his grandfathers injur'd grave, join'd with his murtherers and the abhorr'd betrayers of his country, and plac'd himself at the head of that very party who had trampled on the blood of his family as well as nation. He was in temper brave but rash, had more courage than generosity, more passion than prudence, and more regard to his resentment than to his honour; he was proud without merit, ambitious without prospect, revengeful without injury; he would resent without affront, and quarrel without cause, would embroil himself without reason, and come out of it without honour. His courage was rather in his blood than in his head, and as his actions run often before his thoughts, so his thoughts often run before his reason; yet he was pushing and that supply'd very much his want of policy. But he discover'd the errors of his judgment by the warmth of his behaviour: in every thing he did he sought no disguise, every man knew him better than himself, and he never could be in a plot because he conceal'd nothing. . . .

He has rashness without courage, fury without honour, passion without judgment, and less regard to his character than to his resentment.

(From Atalantis Major, London, 1711)

MARQUIS OF MONTROSE

Grave without Age, without Experience wise
His distinguish'd modesty and humility in all his publick appearances recommends him to the affections of the whole country; and tho' the fortunes of his family have suffered by the disasters of the times, yet he supports a handsome figure suitable to the dignity of his character, rich without gaiety, great without affectation, plentiful without profusion; letting the world see he knows how and when, and to what pitch to appear, that when he pleases to be at large, he can do it like a wise man, or retrench, he can do it like a prince. It might be said, as a finishing stroke to his character, he is just the reverse of Greeniccio (i.e., the Duke of Argyll); for he is fire without thunder, brave without fury, great without pride, gay without vanity, wise without affectation, knows how to obey and how to command. He knows great things enough to manage them, and is so master of himself as not to let them manage him. He knows how to be a courtier without ambition and to merit favour rather than to seek it. He scorns to push his fortunes over the belly of his principles, ever faithful to himself and by consequence to all

that trust him. He has too great a value for merit to envy it even in his enemy, and too low thoughts of the pride and conceit of men without merit, to approve of it even in his friends.

This noble person appears at the head of the dissenting nobility.[36] Nor does it lessen his zeal for the principles of liberty, or the present establishment of religion in his country, that some of his ancestors, otherwise noble, brave and great, appear'd on the other side, since the liberties of his country are the centre of his actions, and the prosperity of all men the mark he aims at.

(*Atalantis Major*, London, 1711)

LORD BELHAVEN

He was a person of nobility, of disposition as well as title, of sence, manners and vertue, of honesty, sobriety and religion, of courage, learning and loyalty; besides being master of a great many good qualities, he had an excellent temper, goodness of disposition, and clearness of judgement above most men; he had an easie conception, a beauty of thought, and a readiness of expression.

In his whole life he shew'd himself zealous for the Protestant religion, the prosperity of his country, and the suppressing of tyranny. And except in the affair of the Union, to which he was entirely averse, and which was the only occasion of his being rendred suspected to the government, his whole life does not show one action but what stiles him the denomination of a true friend to the present government. And yet even in this case he confin'd his disposition to what was legal; and that noble simily his lordship made *ex tempore* after the Union was finish'd shew'd the extent of his design, when being ask'd by one, why he appear'd so easie now it was done. Nay, nay, says he, I have done my part. I was like David in the case of his son: while the child was sick, he fasted, and lay on his face, and shewed his sorrow; but when the child was dead, he washed himself, and put on his garments, and sat down to meat. While the Union was making, I opposed it, and struggled with it, as I thought it my duty; but now it is past, I can do no more. I shall be easie. Again in a letter I have by me from his lordship, there is this expression: I am not, says my lord, going to persuade you to be an anti-Unioner. Since the thing being done, I myself am become a Unioner, as all peaceable subjects ought to be.

In short, he was only unhappy in being suspected by the government, all which was owing to the surface of his conduct in the affair of the Union; and the government could not judge how far anti-Union principles might carry any man, and therefore are to be justified in securing him with others. But he has a perfect loyalty to the Queen, a steady principle for the Revolution, and a zealous heart for the Protestant religion.

(Review, 10 July 1708)

WILLIAM PATERSON
(founder of the Bank of England and the Darien Scheme)

That gentleman is full of calculates, figures, and unperforming numbers, but I see nothing he has done here, nor does anybody else speak of him but in terms I care not to repeat.

(Letter to Harley, 26 November 1706)

JOHN WHITE
(the Edinburgh Hangman)

We had in former times, one John [White] who had the honour to be his Majesty's hangman in this city. This good man had a most gentle easie way of executing his office; for when the poor people came into his hands, and were to die by his operations as many honest men did in those cruel days (this by the way was home to his Lordship, for that this very John cut of his Lordship's grandfather's head), all the while he was a fitting things for the execution of his office, he would smile upon them, talk kindly to them, bid them not be afraid. "Come, come, fear nothing, trust God," and the like. Then bringing them to the foot of the ladder, he would still say, "Be not afraid, come, come, fear nothing, step up one step, do not fear, trust in God", and so to another step and another; and just thus he carried 'em on, till at last with the very words in his mouth, "Fear nothing", he turn'd them off.

(From *Atalantis Major*, 1711)

TOURING SCOTLAND

Finally, towards the end of his life, Defoe brought together his traveller's impressions of Scotland, derived from various trips and tours earlier in his life, and presented them in the third volume of his *Tour through the Whole Island of Great Britain*, published 1726-7. He describes the impression an Englishman receives on first setting foot in Scotland, travelling up the east coast. He views the cities of Edinburgh and Glasgow from various perspectives before presenting a guided tour around the streets and buildings. While he admires Edinburgh's stately architecture, he pronounces Glasgow to be the more beautiful and better-built city of the two.

He takes pleasure in introducing the 'real Caledonia' to his armchair tourists, the Highlands. lochs and rivers, as well as the towns and villages

Much of this territory may be 'frightful country', teeming with wild deer and salmon, and inhabited by even wilder inhabitants, yet he is generous in his praise of the hospitality of Highland chiefs, though he advises tourists to take their own tents so they need not impose too much on the generosity of their hosts. He praises Scotland's eagles and declares that the hawks are the finest in the kingdom.

ARRIVING IN SCOTLAND

I am now just entered Scotland, and that by the ordinary way from Berwick. We tread upon Scots ground after about three miles riding beyond Berwick. The little district between, they say, is neither in England or Scotland, and is call'd Berwickshire, as being formerly a dependant upon the town of Berwick; but we find no towns in it, only straggling farm houses, and one sees the Tweed on one side, which fetches a reach northward, the sea on the other, and the land between lies so high that in stormy weather 'tis very bleak and unpleasant; however, the land is good, and compar'd to our next view, we ought to think very well of it. . . .

Mordintown lying to the west, the great road does not lie thro' it but carries us to the brow of a very high hill where we had a large view into Scotland. But we were welcom'd into it with such a Scots gale of wind that, besides the steepness of the hill, it obliged us to quit our horses for real apprehensions of being blown off, the wind blowing full north, it blew directly in our faces. And I can truly say, I never was sensible of so fierce a wind, so exceeding keen and cold, for it pierc'd our very eyes, that we could scarcely bear to hold them open.

When we came down the hill, the strength of the wind was not felt so much, and consequently not the cold. The first town we come to is as perfectly Scots as if you were 100 miles north off

Edinburgh; nor is there the least appearance of any thing English, either in customs, habits, usages of the people, or in their way of living, eating, dress, or behaviour, any more than if they had never heard of an English nation. Nor was there an Englishman to be seen, or any English family to be found among them.

On the contrary, you have in England abundance of Scotsmen, Scots customs, words, habits, and usages, even more than becomes them; nay, even the buildings in the towns and villages imitate the Scots all over Northumberland. . . .

We pass'd a bridge over the little River Eye, at the mouth of which there is a small harbour with a town call'd Eyemouth, or as some call it, Heymouth. . . .

From this bridge we enter upon a most desolate and, in winter, a most frightful moor for travellers, especially strangers, call'd Condingham or, to speak properly, Coldingham Moor, upon which, for about eight miles, you see hardly a hedge or a tree except in one part, and that at good distance. Nor do you meet with but one house in all the way and that no house of entertainment, which we thought was but a poor reception for Scotland to give her neighbours who were strangers at their very first entrance into her bounds. . . .

Having pass'd this desart, which indeed makes a stranger think Scotland a terrible place, you come down a very steep hill into the Lothains, so the counties are divided, and they are spoken of in plural; because as Yorkshire is divided into the East and West Riding, so here is the East, and West, and Mid Lothain, or Louthain, and therefore justly called Lothains in the plural.

From the top of this hill you begin to see that Scotland is not all desart; and the low lands, which then show themselves, give you a prospect of a fruitful and pleasant country. . . .

EDINBURGH

I am now at the gates of Edinburgh; but before I come to describe the particulars of that city, give me leave to take it in perspective, and speak something of its situation, which will be very necessary with respect to some disadvantage which the city lyes under on that account.

When you stand at a small distance and take a view of it from the east, you have really but a confus'd idea of the city because the situation being in length from east to west, and the breadth but ill proportion'd to its length, you view under the greatest disadvantage possible; whereas if you turn a little to the right hand towards Leith, and so come towards the city from the north, you see a very handsome prospect of the whole city; and from the south you have yet a better view of one part, because the city is encreased on that side with new streets which, on the north side, cannot be.

The particular situation then of the whole is thus. At the extremity of the east end of the city stands the palace or court call'd Haly Rood House; and you must fetch a little sweep to the right hand to leave the palace on the left, and come at the entrance which is call'd the Water Port, and which you come at thro' a short suburb; then bearing to the left again, south, you come to the gate of the palace which faces the great street.

From the palace west the street goes on in almost a straight line and for near a mile and a half in length, some say full two measur'd miles, thro' the whole city to the castle, including the going up the castle in the inside. This is, perhaps, the largest, longest, and finest street for buildings and number of inhabitants, not in Britain only, but in the world. . . .

Here they had had a noble, a pleasant, and a most useful situation, a very fine harbour for their trade, a good road in the firth for their ships of burthen, a pleasant river which, with small art or charge, might have been so drawn round the city as to have fill'd its ditches, and made its fortifications as impregnable

North Prospect of Edinburgh by John Slezer c. 1690 (1719)
Courtesy of Edinburgh City Libraries

as the two loughs did the city, and as the French, when they fortify'd Leith, found easy to do. Or, had they gone to the south side of the city, beyond the deep lough which they say it was, and which is now call'd the Cow-Gate, and extended the city towards Libertoun, and towards good trees, where now stands the delightful seat of Sir James Stuart, late Lord Advocate of Scotland, and the ancient seat of Craigmiller, the seat of Sir Alexander [Gilmour] of Craigmiller, here had been a plain large enough to have contain'd a second London, and water'd on the south part with a pleasant brook sufficient, by the help of pipes, to have carried water into every street and every house. . . .

Having thus considered the city in its appearance and in its present situation, I must look next into its inside, where we shall find it under all its discouragements and disadvantages (and labouring with whatever inconveniencies), a large, populous, noble, rich, and even still a royal city. The main street, as above, is the most spacious, the longest, and best inhabited street in Europe. Its length I have describ'd; the buildings all surprizing both for strength, for beauty, and for height; all, or the greatest part, of free stone and so firm is every thing made, that tho' in so high a situation and in a country where storms and winds are so frequent, 'tis very rare that any damage is done here. No blowing of tiles about the streets to knock people on the head as they pass; no stacks of chimneys and gable ends of houses falling in to bury the inhabitants in their ruins, as we often find it in London and other of our paper built cities in England; but all is fixed, and strong to the top, tho' you have in that part of the city called the Parliament Close houses which, on the south side, appear to be eleven or twelve story high and inhabited to the very top.

From the palace gate westward, this street is called the Cannon-gate, vulgarly the Cannigate, which part, tho' a suburb, is a kind of corporation by itself, as Westminister to London; and has a toll-booth, a prison, and a town guard by itself, tho' under the government of the provost and bailiffs of Edinburgh, as Leith itself also is. In this part of the street, tho' otherwise not so well inhabited as the city itself, are several very magnificent houses of the nobility, built for their residence when the court was in town, and on their other occasions. . . .

We now enter the city, properly so called. In almost the first buildings of note on the north side of the street, the Marquess of Tweedale has a good city house, with a plantation of lime-trees behind it instead of a garden, the place not allowing room for a large garden; adjoining to which are very good buildings, tho' in the narrow wynds and alleys, such as if set out in handsome streets would have adorn'd a very noble city but are here crouded together, as may be said, without notice.

Here the physicians have a hall, and adjoining to it a very good garden; but I saw no simples[37] in it of value, there being a physick garden at the palace which furnishes them sufficiently. But they have a fine musaeum, or chamber of rarities, which are worth seeing and which, in some things, is not to be match'd in Europe. Dr Belford, afterwards knighted, began the collection.

Sir Robert Sibbald has printed a catalogue of what was then deposited in his time. The physicians of Edinburgh have preserved the character of able, learned and experienced, and have not been outdone by any of their neighbours; and the late Dr Pitcairn, who was the Ratcliff of Scotland, has left large testimonies of his skill in nature and medicine to the world.

It must not be expected I can go on to describe all the buildings of the city; I shall therefore only touch at such things, and go on. From the Neither Bow, you have an open view up the High Street. On the south side is the Trone Kirk, and a little farther, in the middle of the street the Guard House, where the town guard does duty every night. These are in the stead of our watchmen, and the town maintains two full companies of them, clothed and armed as grenadiers.

Those are as a guard to keep the publick peace of the city, but I cannot but acknowledge that they are not near so good a safe guard to the citizens against private robberies as our watchmen in London are; and Edinburgh is not without such fellows as shop lifters, house-robbers, and pick pockets in proportion to the number of people, as much as London itself. . . .

About midway between the Nether Bow and the Castle Hill is the great church; formerly it was called the cathedral, and was all one church dedicated to St Giles. On the south side of this church is a square of very fine buildings, which is called by the name of the Parliament Close; the west side of the square, and part of the south, is taken up with the Parliament House, and the several Courts of Justice, the Council Chamber, the Treasury, the publick offices, registers, the publick library &c, the Court for the meeting of the Royal Buroughs and several offices needful when the independency of Scotland was in being, but now not so much in use. But as the Session or College of Justice, the Exchequer, and the Justiciary or Courts for Criminal Causes still exist, the usual places for their assembling are still preserved. These buildings are very fine, all of free stone, well finish'd, and very magnificent. The great church makes up the north side of the square, and the east remaining part of the south side is built into private dwellings very stately, lofty, and strong, being seven story high to the front of the square, and the hill they stand on giving so sudden a descent, they are eleven or twelve s[tor]y high backward. . . .

The great opening into the High Street, being the only passage into it for coaches, is at the north east corner between the south east corner of the High Kirk and the opposite high buildings, and a little from the opening is the Market Cross where all their proclamations and publick acts are read and publish'd by sound of trumpet. Here is the great parade where every day the gentlemen meet for business or news, as at an exchange; the usual time of meeting is from eleven to one. Here is also another passage at the north west corner which goes into the Land Market, and another passage down innumerable stone stairs, on the south side, leading to the Cowgate.

On the west end of the great church, but in a different building, is the Tolbooth or common prison, as well for criminals as debtors, and a miserable hole it is, to say no worse of it. . . . [T]hose buildings past, the street opens again to a breadth rather wider than before, and is called the Land Market, but for what reason I know not.[38] This part is nobly built, and extends west to the Castle Hill, or rather to a narrower street which leads up to the Castle.

At the upper end of this Land Market is a stone building appropriated to several publick offices of lesser value, and is called the weigh-house, for below stairs are warehouses with publick weights and scales for heavy goods.

Here the High Street ends, and parting into two streets, one goes away south west and descending gradually leads by the West Bow, as 'tis called, to the Grass-market. This street which is called the Bow, is generally full of wholesale traders and those very considerable dealers in iron, pitch, tar, oyl, hemp, flax, linseed, painters colours, dyers, drugs, and woods, and such like heavy goods, and supplies country shopkeepers as our wholesale dealers in England do. And here I may say, is a visible face of trade; most of them have also warehouses in Leith, where they lay up the heavier goods and bring them hither, or sell them by patterns and samples, as they have occasion. . . .

The markets in Edinburgh are not in the open street, except that in the High Street where there is every morning an herb and fruit market which yet abates before noon, and what remains then is no grievance. Besides this, there are several distinct market places wall'd in and reserved for the particular things they are appointed for, and very well regulated by the magistrates, and well supplied also, as:

The meal market.
The flesh market.
The poultry market.
The butter-market.
The grass-market   } kept open, and in the same
                                      street just within
       horse-market   } the West Port

with several others. There is also in the street called the Land Market a weekly market for all sorts of woollen manufactures, and some mercery and drapery goods, and also for linnen cloth.

GLASGOW

I am now cross'd the Clyde to Glasgow, and I went over dry-footed without the bridge; on which occasion I cannot but observe how differing a face the river presented itself in, at those two several times when only I was there. At the first, being in the

View of Glasgow from Fir Park by John Slezer c. 1690,
courtesy of Glasgow City Libraries

month of June, the river was so low that not the horses and carts
only pass'd it just above the bridge, but the children and boys
playing about went every where, as if there was no river, only
some little spreading brook, or wash, like such as we have at
Enfield-Wash or Chelston Wash in Middlesex; and, as I told you,
cross'd it dry-foot, that is, the water was scarce over the horses
hoofs.

As for the bridge, which is a lofty stately fabrick, it stood out
of the water as naked as a skeleton and looked somewhat like the
bridge over the Manfanares near Madrid, which I mentioned
once before; of which a French ambassador told the people the
king should either buy them a river or sell their bridge; or like
the stone bridge at Chester in the Street in Northumberland,
where the road goes in the river and the people ride under the
bridge in dry weather instead of riding over it. So when I saw
such a magnificent bridge at Glasgow, and especially when I saw
three of the middle arches so exceeding large and high beyond
all the rest, I could not but wonder, hardly thinking it possible
that where the passage or channel is so exceeding broad, for the

bridge consists of eight arches, the river which in its ordinary channel is so narrow as it is higher up and at a distance from it, could ever fill up such a height, where it has so grand a space to spread itself as at the bridge.

But my next journey satisfy'd me when, coming into Glasgow from the east side, I found the river not only had filled up all the arches of the bridge but, running about the end of it, had fill'd the streets of all that part of the city next the bridge to the infinite damage of the inhabitants, besides putting them into the greatest consternation imaginable for fear of their houses being driven away by the violence of the water; and the whole city was not without apprehensions that their bridge would have given way too, which would have been a terrible loss to them, for 'tis as fine a bridge as most in Scotland.

Glasgow is, indeed, a very fine city. The four principal streets are the fairest for breadth and the finest built that I have ever seen in one city together. The houses are all stone, and generally equal and uniform in height as well as in front. The lower story generally stands on vast square dorick columns, not round pillars, and arches between give passage into the shops adding to the strength as well as beauty of the building. In a word, 'tis the cleanest and beautifullest and best built city in Britain, London excepted.

It stands on the side of a hill, sloping to the river, with this exception, that the part next the river is flat, as is said above, for near one third part of the city, and that exposed it to the water upon the extraordinary flood mention'd just now.

Where the streets meet, the crossing makes a spacious market place by the nature of the thing, because the streets are so large of themselves. As you come down the hill from the north gate to the said Cross, the Tolbooth, with the Stad-house or Guild-Hall, make the north east angle or, in English, the right-hand corner of the street, the building very noble and very strong ascending by large stone steps with an iron balustrade. Here the town-council sit and the magistrates try causes, such as come within their cognizance, and do all their publick business.

On the left hand of the same street is the University. The building is the best of any in Scotland of the kind; it was founded by Bishop Turnbull ann. 1454 but has been much enlarged since, and the fabrick almost all new built. It is a very spacious building, contains two large squares or courts, and the lodgings for the scholars and for the professors are very handsome. The whole building is of freestone, very high and very august. Here is a Principal, with regents and professors in every science, as there is at Edinburgh, and the scholars wear gowns, which they do not at Edinburgh. Their gowns here are red, but the Masters of Arts and Professors wear black gowns, with a large cape of velvet to distinguish them.

The Cathedral is an antient building and has a square tower in the middle of the Cross with a very handsome spire upon it, the highest that I saw in Scotland and, indeed, the only one that is to be called high. This, like St Giles's at Edinburgh, is divided now, and makes three churches and, I suppose, there is four or five more in the city, besides a meeting[39] or two. But there are very few of the Episcopal Dissenters here; and the mob fell upon one of their meetings so often that they were obliged to lay it down or, if they do meet, 'tis very privately.

THE REAL CALEDONIA

I am now to enter the true and real Caledonia, for the country on the north of the firth [of Forth] is alone called by that name, and was antiently known by no other. As I shall give an account of it as it is, and not as it was, so I shall describe it as I view'd it, not as other people have view'd it; nor shall I confine my self to the division of the country, as the geographers have divided it, or to the shires and counties, as the civil authority has divided it, or into presbyteries and synodical provinces, as the church has divided it. But noting the shires where I find them needful, I shall give an account of things in the order of my own progress and as I pass'd thro' or visited them.

MONTROSE

The town and port of Montrose, vulgarly but ignorantly called Montross, was our next stage, standing upon the eastmost shore of Angus, open to the German or, if you please, now the Caledonian Ocean, and at the mouth of the little River South Esk which makes the harbour.

We did not find so kind a reception among the common people of Angus and the other shires on this side the country, as the Scots usually give to strangers; but we found it was because we were English men; and we found that their aversion did not lye so much against us on account of the late successes at and after the Rebellion, and the forfeiture of the many noblemen and

Montrose, an inset from Herman Moll, *The North Part of Britain called Scotland* (1714), reproduced by permission of the Trustees of the National Library of Scotland

gentlemen's estates among them as fell on that occasion, though that might add to the disgust; but it was on account of the Union, which they almost universally exclaimed against, tho' sometimes against all manner of just reasoning.

This town of Montrose is a sea port and, in proportion to its number of inhabitants, a considerable trade, and is tolerably well built and capable of being made strong, only that it extends too far in length.

The French fleet first made land at this port, when they had the Pretender on board in the reign of Queen Ann, having overshot the mouth of the firth so far, whither they had first designed. But this mistake, which some thought a misfortune, was certainly a deliverance to them, for as this mistake gave time to the English fleet to come up with them before they could enter the firth, so it left them time and room also to make their escape which, if they had been gone up the firth, they could never have done but must inevitably have been all burnt and destroyed, or taken by the British fleet under Sir George Bing, which was superior to them in force.

LOCH NESS & INVERNESS

From the western part of this country you may observe that the land goes away again to the north and, as if you were to enter into another island beyond Britain, you find a large lake or inlet from the Sea of Murray, mention'd above, going on west, as if it were to cut through the island, for we could see no end of it; . . . we perceived the lake contracted in one particular place to the ordinary size of a river, as if design'd by nature to give passage to the inhabitants to converse[40] with the northern part, and then, as if that part had been sufficiently perform'd, it open'd again to its former breadth and continued in the form of a large lake as before for many more miles than we could see, being in the whole, according to Mr Cambden, twenty-three miles long; but if it be taken on both sides the pass, 'tis above thirty-five miles in length. . . .

In the narrow pass (mention'd above) over the lake stands the town and fortress of Inner-Ness, that is, a town on the inner bank of the River Ness. The situation of it, as I have said before, intimates that it is a place for strength, and accordingly it has a castle, founded in antient times to command the pass; and some authors write that it was antiently a royal house for the kings of Scotland. Be that as it will, Oliver Cromwell thought it a place of such importance that he built a strong citadel here and kept a stated garrison always in it, and sometimes more than a garrison, finding it needful to have a large body of his old veteran troops posted here to preserve the peace of the country and keep the Highlands in awe, which they did effectually all his time. . . .

The fort which was then built and since demolished, has been restored since the Revolution, and a garrison was always kept here by King William for the better regulating the Highlands; and this post was of singular importance in the time of the late insurrection of the Lord Marr for the Pretender when, though his party took it, they were driven out again by the country with the assistance of the Earl of Sutherland and several other of the nobility and gentry who stood fast to the king's interest.

Here is a stately stone bridge of seven large arches over the River Ness. . . .

When you are over this bridge you enter that which we truly call the North of Scotland, and others the North Highlands, in which are several distinct shires, but cannot call for a distinct description because it is all one undistinguish'd range of mountains and woods, overspread with vast and almost uninhabited rocks and steeps, fill'd with deer innumerable and of a great many kinds, among which are some of those the antients called harts and roebucks, with vast overgrown stags and hinds of the red deer kind, and with fallow deer also.

And here, before I describe this frightful country, it is needful to observe that Scotland may be thus divided into four districts or distinct quarters which, however, I have not seen any of our geographers do before me, yet, I believe, may not be an improper measurement for such as would form a due idea of the whole in their minds, as follows:

1. The South Land, or that part of Scotland south of the River Tay, drawing a line from the Tay, about Perth, to Loch Lomond, and down again to Dumbarton and the Bank of Clyde.

2. The Middle, or Midland, being all the country from the Tay and the Lough Lomon, north to the Lake of Ness and the Aber, including a long slope to the south, taking in the western Highlands of Argyle and Lorn, and the Isles of Isla and Iura.

3. The North Land, being all the country beyond Innerness and the Lough, or River Ness, north drawing the line over the narrow space of Glengary, between the Ness and the Aber, and bounded by them both from the eastern to the western sea.

4. The Islands, being all the western and northern islands (viz.) the Hebrides, the Skye, the Orkneys, and the Isles of Shetland.

Upon the foot of this division I am now, having pass'd the bridge over the Ness, enter'd upon the third division of Scotland, called the North Land; and it is of this country that, as I am saying, the mountains are so full of deer, harts, roe bucks, &c.

Here are also a great number of eagles which breed in the woods, and which prey upon the young fawns when they first fall. Some of these eagles are of a mighty large kind, such as are not to be seen again in those parts of the world.

Here are also the best hawks of all the kinds for sport which are in the kingdom, and which the nobility and gentry of Scotland make great use of; for not this part of Scotland only, but all the rest of the country abounds with wild fowl.

The rivers and lakes also in all this country are prodigiously full of salmon. It is hardly credible what the people relate of the quantity of salmon taken in these rivers, especially in the Spey, the Nairn, the Ness, and other rivers thereabout. . . .

All the country beyond this river, and the loch flowing in it, is call'd Caithness, and extends to the northermost land in Scotland.

JOHN O' GROATS TO SKYE

I am now to observe that we are here at the extremest end or point of the island of Great Britain; and that here the land bears away west, leaving a large strait or sea, which they call Pentland Firth, and which divides between the island of Great Britain and the Isles of the Orkneys, a passage broad and fair, for 'tis not less than five leagues over and with a great depth of water, so that any ships or fleets of ships may go thro' it. But the tides are so fierce, so uncertain, and the gusts and suddain squals of wind so frequent, that very few merchants-ships care to venture thro' it; and the Dutch East India ships, which come north about (as 'tis called) in their return from India, keep all farther off, and choose to come by Fair Isle, that is to say, in the passage between the Islands of Orkney and Shetland. . . .

In the passage between the Land's End of Britain and the Orkneys is a small island, which our mariners call Stroma, Mr Cambden and others Sowna; 'tis spoken much of as dangerous for ships, but I see no room to record any thing of that kind any more than that there are witches and spirits haunting it, which draw ships on shore to their misfortunes. Such things I leave to the people who are of the opinion the devil has such retreats for doing mischief; for my own part I believe him employed in business of more moment.

As Dingsby Head is the most northerly land of Great Britain, 'tis worth observing to you that here, in the month of June, we had so clear an uninterrupted day that, though indeed the sun does set, that is to say, the horizon covers its whole body for some hours, yet you might see to read the smallest print and to write distinctly, without the help of a candle or any other light, and that all night long. . . .

From hence west we go along the shore of the firth or passage, which they call Pentland; and here is the house so famous, called John a Grot's house, where we set our horses feet into the sea, on the most northerly land, as the people say, of Britain, though, I think, Dungsby Head is as far north. 'Tis certain, however, the difference is but very small, being either of them in the latitude of 59 16th North, and Shetland reaching above two degrees farther. The dominions of Great Britain are extended from the Isle of Wight, in the latitude of 50 degrees, to the Isles of Unsta in Shetland, in the latitude of 61 degrees, 30 minutes, being ten degrees, or full 660 miles in length; which Island of Unst or Unsta being the most remote of the Isles of Shetland to the north east, lyes 167 leagues from Winterton Ness in Norfolk.

Here we found however mountainous and wild the country appeared, the people were extremely well furnished with provisions; and especially they had four sorts of provisions in great plenty, and with a supply of which 'tis reasonable to say they could suffer no dangerous want:

1. Very good bread, as well oat bread as wheat, though the last so cheap as the first.

2. Venison exceeding plentiful, and at all seasons, young or old, which they kill with their guns wherever they find it; for there is no restraint, but 'tis every man's own that can kill it. By which means the Highlanders not only have all of them fire arms, but they are all excellent marksmen.

3. Salmon in such plenty as is scarce credible and so cheap that to those who have any substance to buy with, it is not worth

their while to catch it themselves. This they eat fresh in the season, and for other times they cure it by drying it in the sun, by which they preserve it all the year.

They have no want of cows and sheep, but the latter are so wild that sometimes were they not by their own disposition use to flock together, they would be much harder to kill than the deer. . . .

We therefore turned our faces to the south, and with great satisfaction after so long and fatiguing a journey; and unless we had been assisted by the gentlemen of the country and with very good guides, it had been next to an impossibility to have pass'd over this part of the country. I do confess if I was to recommend to any men whose curiosity tempted them to travel over this part of the country the best method for their journeying, it should be neither to seek towns, for it would be impossible to find such in proper stages for their journey, nor to make themselves always burthensome to the Highland chiefs, tho' there I can assure them they would always meet with great treatment and great hospitality.

But I would propose travelling with some company and carrying tents with them, and so encamping every night as if they were an army. . . .

Here we found the town of Tain and some other villages tollerably well inhabited, and some trade also, occasioned principally by the communication with the western islands and also by the herring fishing, the fishing boats from other parts often putting into these ports for all their coast is full of loughs and rivers and other openings which make very good harbours for shipping; and that which is remarkable, some of those loughs are infinitely full of herrings even where, as they tell us, they have no communication with the sea, so that they must have in all probability been put into them alive by some particular hands, and have multiplied there as we find at this time.

We could understand nothing on this side of what the people

said, any more than if we had been in Morocco; and all the remedy we had was that we found most of the gentlemen spoke French, and some few spoke broad Scots. We found it also much for our convenience to make the common people believe we were French. . . .

On this coast is the Isle of Skye, lying from the west north west to the east and bearing upon the main island, only separated by a narrow strait of water, something like as the Isle of Wight is separated from the county of Southampton. We left this on our right, and crossing the mountains came with as little stay as we could to the Lough of Abre, that is, the water which as I said above, assists with Lough Mess, or Loch Ness, to separate the north land of Scotland from the middle part.

This is a long and narrow inlet of the sea which opening from the Irish Sea S. West meets the River Abre, or as the Scots much more properly express it, the Water of Abre, for it is rather a large lake or loch than a river . . .

[A]ll that mountainous barren and frightful country which lies south of the Water of Abre is called Loquabre, or the country bordering on Loch Abre. It is indeed a frightful country, full of hidious desart mountains and unpassable except to the Highlanders who possess the precipices. Here in spight of the most vigorous pursuit, the Highland robbers such as the famous Rob Roy in the late disturbances, find such retreats as none can pretend to follow them into, nor could he be ever taken.

On this Water of Abre, just at the entrance of the lock, was anciently a fort built, to curb the Highlanders on either side. It was so situated, that tho' it might indeed be block'd up by land and be destress'd by a siege, the troops besieging being masters of the field, yet as it was open to the sea, it might always receive supplies by shipping, the government being supposed to be always master of the sea, or at least 'tis very probable they will be so.

This fort the late King William caused to be rebuilt, or rather a new fort to be erected, where there was always a good garrison kept for curbing the Highlanders, which fort was for several years commanded by Lieutenant General Maitland. . . .

GRAMPIAN MOUNTAINS

The Grampian Mountains, which are here said to cut through Scotland as the Muscovites say of their Riphaean Hills: they are the girdle of the world. As is the country, so are the inhabitants, a fierce fighting and furious kind of men; but I must add that they are much changed, and civiliz'd from what they were formerly. . . .

It is indeed a very bitter character, and possibly they might deserve it in those days; but I must insist that they are quite another people now. And tho' the country is the same, and the mountains as wild and desolate as ever, yet the people, by the good conduct of their chiefs and heads of clans, are much more civilized than they were in former times.

As the men have the same vigour and spirit but are under a better regulation of their manners and more under government, so they make excellent soldiers when they come abroad, or are listed in regular and disciplin'd troops. . . .

Soon after its first coming out from the mountains, the Earn spreads itself into a loch, as most of those rivers do. . . .

On the bank of this River Earn lies a very pleasant vale which continues from the Tay, where it receives the river quite up to the Highlands. This is called, according to the usage of Scotland, Strath Earn, or the Strath or Vale of Earn. . . .

The Western Highlands

The Western Highlands are the only remaining part of Scotland which as yet I have not toucht upon. This is that particular country which a late great man in King James the Second's time called the kingdom of Argyle. . . . It is true that the greatest part of these Western Highlands may be said to be subject or in some respect to belong to the House of Argyle or, to speake more properly, to the family or clan of the Campbells, of whom the Duke of Argyle is the chief. . . .

But if they will claim the country, they must claim the people too, who are, if I may give my opinion, some of the worst, most barbarous and ill governed of all their Highlands of Scotland. They are desperate in fight, cruel in victory, fierce even in conversation, apt to quarrel, mischievous, and even murderers in their passion. . . .

[W]e went away west, but were presently interrupted by a vast inland sea, rather than a lake, called Loch Lomond. . . . This lake or loch is without comparison the greatest in Scotland; no other can be called half so big, for it is more than twenty miles long and generally eight miles in breadth, though at the north end of it 'tis not so broad by far. It receives many rivers into it, but empties itself into the Firth of Clyde at one mouth. Near the entrance of it into the Clyde stands the famous Dumbarton Castle, the most antient as well as the most important castle in Scotland, and the gate, as 'tis called, of the Highlands.

CONCLUSION

Suffer th'impartial Pen to range thy Shore,
And do thee Justice; Nature asks no more.

– CALEDONIA –

Daniel Defoe went to Edinburgh as a spy in September 1706 and within a few months publicly proclaimed himself 'a lover of Scotland' in the dedication (to the Duke of Queensberry) of his panegyric, *Caledonia*. This poem, subtitled 'A poem in honour of Scotland and the Scots nation', found ready subscribers among Scottish nobles and lords, many of whom were perhaps flattered by verses that named them and their illustrious ancestors. Defoe's audacity knew no bounds, it seems, for he wrote in the same dedication:

All the spies sent hither have carry'd back an ill report of the land, and fill'd the world with weak banters and clamour at they know not what. . . .

When a stranger comes into Scotland, fill'd with those formidable ideas which the enemies of the nation ignorantly and maliciously have form'd in him, he is confounded and asham'd of himself: the cultivated lands, the noble harbours, the numerous villages, the seats of the nobility and gentry, and the plenty of all things are perfect surprizes, and he is apt to enquire whether this be Scotland or no.

He concludes by presenting himself as the very person 'to rescue Scotland out of the jaws of slander'.

Defoe rarely underestimated the power of the word, particularly the power of print, even if he did overstate his own role as Scotland's champion. Words, once broadcast, could be misunderstood, as he found to his cost when he was imprisoned and pilloried for one tract about the treatment of the Dissenters, and arrested for supposedly Jacobite sympathies expressed in others. Defoe's publications, especially his *Review* articles from Edinburgh, were also used against him, by fellow writers, as the following extract from an 'open letter' to Defoe from an anonymous English wit illustrates:

Daniel,

You have found by long Experience, that a Prophet has no Reputation in his own Country, and that made you take a Tour to the Northward, where, in the ancient Kingdom, you have gain'd (as you say) such a wonderful Applause, as never the like was known.

But People can hardly believe what you say: For when I tell 'em your own Story, That some Merchants have employ'd you to contract for ten thousand Pounds in Salt Yearly, they answer me with all the Derision in the World, He buy ten thousand Pounds of Salt! He buy ten thousand T—s. And, old Friend, it seems something strange that you who, when you were here, could not be trusted for ten Pence, should now when you are abroad, be trusted for ten thousand Pounds, when the People may easily be inform'd of your Character!

Others, mitigating the Matter, say, that you han't left your old Wont of equivocating; and that by ten thousand Pounds, you mean ten thousand Pounds Scots, at twenty pence to the Pound; but most believe you have a Mind to cheat Somebody. *Caveat Scotus.* For *English*-men know you.

> (*The Review Review'd. In a Letter to the Prophet Daniel in Scotland*, London, 1707)

While such attacks in print were common enough at the time, Defoe may have endured more than his fair share of them. His failed commercial enterprises, bankruptcies, prolific 'scribbling', and seeming readiness to use his pen as his political masters directed, were all publicised by enemies and rivals. Inevitably, the lengthy periods he spent in Scotland, and his extensive writing about Scottish affairs, drew criticism. He found himself mocked for his scotticisms and lampooned for his vanity:

Here is muckle ado anent thy being in Scotland, who ar't the Life and Soul of the modern *Whigs*; . . . I would advise thee to give over thy Proposal of Printing thy History of the Union; . . . I don't think thou wil't get any Subscriptions: But if the People are so foolish when 'tis printed, don't put thy horrid Phiz before it, to fright the Children in the Title Page; there will be Nonsense enough in the Book to disturb the Men.

(The Review Review'd)

Defoe responded to such 'scurrilous prints and scandalous reproaches' by scorning his detractors: 'rail on, gentlemen, the dirt you throw flyes back in your own faces, and bears me sufficient testimony that the physick works well, by the vomit and stink of the patients' (*Review*, 13 May 1707).

Sometimes he cited specific caustic comments, or published hostile letters in his periodical; sometimes he took satisfaction in quoting the favourable remarks of more respected--and respectful--opponents, like Lord Belhaven, for instance, whose famous anti-Union speech Defoe had once satirised in print.

His Lordship's Words are these:
I confess, I thought you gave yourself too much liberty in bantering me and my speech in your writings, especially in your Introduction to that of my Lord H[aversha]ms; yet by what I

have seen of your other writings, you are of the same sentiments with me as to government, &c, and, except in the matter of Union, you are a man after my own heart.

And I am so well pleased with some of your last Review, with relation to the affairs of Scotland, and particularly your aenigma or allegory of the widow, that I freely forgive you all your former sins of ignorance.

(*Review*, 10 July 1708)

Few of Defoe's political opponents were as forgiving as Belhaven. These utterly disparaging verses are more typical:

A fawning, canting, double hearted Knave
Is the inscription fittest for his Grave.
Look there's the Bribes with which this Wretch was paid
When he this Country and its Right betray'd.

Lo that False Vizard which this K[nave] put on;
Wrote one day *Pro* and th'other day writ *[C]on*.
There's no such *Proteus* to be found in Story,
One hour a *Whig* and the next hour a *Tory*.
Sometimes Dissenter and sometimes High Church
Strait turns his Coat leaves both sides in the Lurch.
He wrote for all cause that did yield him most.[41]

This indictment appeared in Read's *Weekly Journal*, a rival paper to Mist's *Weekly-Journal*, or *Saturday's Evening Post* for which Defoe was writing by 1717. Nathaniel Mist was a well-known Jacobite journalist, and Defoe was actually working as a secret agent again, this time paid by the new Whig government to infiltrate Mist's Tory, anti-Hanoverian newspaper. Defoe's job was to 'take the sting' out of this very popular paper.

While it is hard to know which particular articles Defoe contributed to *The Weekly-Journal*, a change in tone can be found soon after he became one of the writers. His hand is detectable in this leader published on 3 August, 1717 (when Mist was under arrest on suspicion of seditious libel):

They [the authors of the paper] desire to live peaceably and inoffensively, in a due and full submission to the present government, in loyalty to King George, and observance of the established laws of their country; they move no sedition, or rebellion, nor were ever concerned in any such thing, or with those that were, the work being now under different hands from those which some people have suggested it to be.

Like other newspapers of the day, Mist's *Weekly-Journal* covered both foreign and domestic news, including regular reports from Scotland. Defoe's main responsibility was to translate foreign dispatches. Before he joined the paper, Mist's Jacobite bias is evident, as in this leader from 15 June, 1717:

Our last letters from Rome give the following account of the magnificent reception of the Chevalier de St George in that city. . . . The Chevalier (whom they gave the title of King) went to see the Basilique or Church of St Peter with a numerous train of coaches. . . . [H]e was conducted to an audience of the Pope . . . and after the usual compliments was seated in a great two-armed chair enriched with crimson velvet, and a gold fringe. He was entertained there two entire hours, after which he was re-conducted with the same ceremonies and the same treatment done to the Emperor Charles the Fifth.

(*The Weekly-Journal*, no. 27)

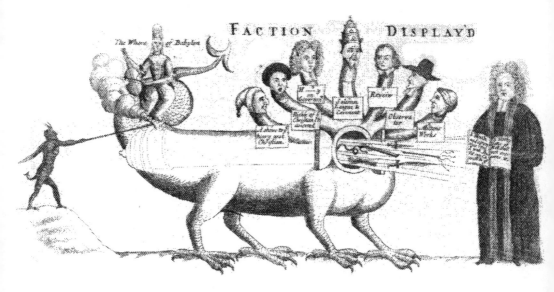

Faction Display'd, by permission of the British Library (C.121.g.9/112).
This contemporary cartoon depicts Sir Robert Harley and Daniel
Defoe as two of the seven heads of the beast of the Apocalypse.
Harley is on the left and Defoe on the right of the mitred head of
'Popery' (Defoe is labelled 'Review')

The report from Edinburgh in the same issue notes that Rob Roy
MacGregor 'the famous Highland partisan, last week surrendered himself to
the Duke of Athol'. Then the edition of 22 June advises that, while the duke
awaited orders as to what he should do with his prisoner, Rob Roy 'walk'd
back again in the meanwhile to the hills, without giving the least notice of
his departure'.

News of Rob Roy's latest raids and evasion of re-capture continued to
feature quite regularly in *The Weekly-Journal*, suggesting fascination with
the subject and sometimes a sneaking admiration for his exploits. In
December, however, with Mist in custody again, a cynical ballad, 'A Race at
Sheriff-Muir', which poked fun at the inconclusive battle that ended the 1715
Jacobite Rebellion, appeared in his paper with this equivocal introduction:

The following ballad we had some time by us, coming by the post from Scotland; we think it very hard that such innocent things as these, full of meer mirth and humour, should require any introduction; and were it not that the malice of Mr St James's Post[42] and Mr Read, the Protestant journal-monger, makes such a pother about us, there could be no room for any apology for now and then a ballad. As for the song, we see no harm in it, and mean none.

(*The Weekly-Journal*, Saturday, 21 December, 1717)

The opening lines and chorus of this ballad survive in popular Scottish folksongs:

There's some say that we wan, and some say that they wan,
Some say that nane wan at au – Man

The version that Defoe probably had a hand in printing includes a verse that does not appear in later versions, and may betray a Hanoverian bias:[43]

Rob Roy stood at watch, on a hill for to catch
 The booty, for ought that I saw – Man;
For he ne'er advanct from the place he was stanct,
 Till no more was to do there at aw – man.

 For we ran, and they ran, &c.

Apart from a short interval at the end of 1718, Defoe wrote for Mist's *Weekly-Journal* until 1724. During this same period, he embarked on yet another career – novel-writing – producing six novels in five years, not to mention two sequels to *Robinson Crusoe*.

Two of his novels, as we have seen, reflect to some degree his abiding interest in Scots and Scotland, but it was in the final volume of his *Tour of the Whole Island of Great Britain*, published in 1726, that he was able to 'return' to Scotland, through an imaginative re-enactment of his own early journeys and experiences north of the border.

SEE INTRO. TO TRAVOUS BOOK

Notes

[1] For the background to this, see Christopher A. Whatley, *Bought and Sold for English Gold?* (Tuckwell Press, 2001).

[2] The rest of the instructions are missing, leaving the disturbing suggestion of threatened consequences.

[3] This is graphically confirmed in contemporary Scottish sources, e.g. the papers of anti-Unionist, George Lockhart of Carnwath.

[4] The Duke of Queensberry.

[5] A torch made of tow and pitch.

[6] Defoe included a copy of Lord Belhaven's speech in his *History of the Union* (1709).

[7] The treaty between England and France signed as part of the Peace of Utrecht on 11 April, 1713, ending the War of the Spanish Succession.

[8] The proclamation referred to was against tumultory meetings.

[9] Defoe does not provide a first name, but in an earlier letter to Harley he identifies Finlay as one of the leaders of the Glasgow rabble (7 December, 1706).

[10] Defoe is referring to the Cameronians.

[11] Pardoned.

[12] This may refer to the suspension of *Habeas Corpus* in order to arrest and detain all Jacobite suspects, or to the 1709 amendment to the Penal Act (1704) which aimed to limit the power and landholdings of Roman Catholics.

[13] This is a reference to the recent election of peers to the British parliament.

[14] Oboes.

[15] Anak was the father of three giants (Jos. 15:13, 14; 21:11).

[16] Dutch troops were brought in to assist the Government army commanded by the Duke of Argyll.

[17] See my Introduction, p. 20, and also Paula R. Backscheider, *Daniel Defoe, His Life* (London, 1989), pp. 206-8.

[18] *Graving*: the cleaning of a ship's bottom by scraping or burning, and coating with tar (OED).

[19] *Caulkers* stopped up the seams of a ship with oakum, and melted pitch or resin to prevent leaking.

20 *Bomb Ketch*: a small ketch-rigged vessel, carrying one or two mortars for bombarding (OED).

21 *Riding*: floating or sailing.

22 than in.

23 *Anglicé*, meaning 'in English'.

24 The settlement of the succession on the House of Hanover, stipulated in article 2 of the Act of Union, deprived James VII and the Stuart line of the crown.

25 See next extract.

26 His *History of the Union*.

27 Maccraw, possibly Macrae, a clan on good terms with the McKenzie chiefs; or Maccraw, a sept of the clan McRae.

28 *Wast-house*: an unoccupied dwelling.

29 Another MacKenzie castle was located here too.

30 Defoe had written to Harley on 27 August, a few days previously, enclosing an account of the Cameronian meeting at Auchsauch Hill which he said he had received from Scotland.

31 i.e. special characteristic or quality.

32 See pp. 154-55.

33 On the edge of Loch Lomond.

34 Duke of Atholl, around 1717.

35 The 1715 Jacobite Rising led by the Earl of Mar.

36 He led the *Squadrone Volante* party.

37 Plants or herbs employed for medical purposes.

38 The *Landmarket*, now known as the Lawnmarket, was the place where produce of the land, or country, was sold at market.

39 Meeting house for dissenters.

40 *Converse*, meaning to have commercial dealings with, to trade.

41 Quoted by Backscheider, *Daniel Defoe*, p. 432.

42 *St James Chronicle* or the *British Evening Post*.

43 Rob Roy's most recent biographer describes this broadside as 'a satirical Hanoverian ballad'. David Stevenson, *Rob Roy: The Man and the Myths* (Edinburgh, 2004), p. 110.

GLOSSARY

Abjuration Repudiation upon oath of the claims to the throne of the house of Stuart, including the descendants of the Pretender, imposed by William III.

Cameronian Member of the sect led by Covenanter Richard Cameron in the 1680s who renounced allegiance to king and government on religious grounds, and subsequently rejected the Revolution Settlement.

Court Party Political party which advocated the interests of the Court, as opposed to the Country Party, which advocated the interests and claims of the country as a whole.

Covenanter Originally, one of those who signed the National Covenant (1638) and Solemn League and Covenant (1643).

Dissenter One who dissented and separated from the national church, in England, the Established Church of England, and in Scotland the Presbyterian Church of Scotland.

Drawbacks An amount of excise or import duty, previously paid, remitted or drawn back when the commodities on which it has been paid are exported.

Equivalent The Equivalent was the sum of money ordered, by the 1707 Act of Union, to be paid to Scotland as a set-off against additional excise duties, loss on coinage, etc.

Incorporation Union in or into one body, as opposed to federation in which each country retains the management of its internal affairs.

Nonjuror Person, usually a beneficed clergyman, who refused to take an oath of allegiance in 1689 to William and Mary and their successors.

Revolution Settlement The religious settlement (1689-90), following their acceptance of the English and Scottish Crowns, whereby William and Mary agreed to adhere to the Protestant faith and Presbyterianism was fully restored in Scotland.

Squadrone Sometimes Squadrone volante. An early eighteenth-century Scottish political party.

Tacker One who advocated tacking the bill against occasional conformity, 1704, to a money-bill.

Toleration Allowance of the exercise of religion other than in the officially established form. The Act of Toleration (1689) granted freedom of religious worship, on certain prescribed conditions, to Dissenting Protestants.

BIBLIOGRAPHY

REFERENCES

Backscheider, Paula R., *Daniel Defoe: His Life,* Baltimore, 1989

Douglas, Hugh, *Jacobite Spy Wars*, Stroud, 1999

Healey, George Harris (ed.), *The Letters of Daniel Defoe*, Oxford, 1955

McKim, Anne M., 'Adapting News and Making History: Defoe and the Union' in *Early Modern News Discourse*, ed., Nicholas Brownlees, New York & Berlin, 2006

Novak, Maximilian, 'A Whiff of Scandal in the Life of Daniel Defoe', *Huntingdon Library Quarterly* (1970), 35-42

Scott, Paul H., *Defoe in Edinburgh and Other Papers*, East Linton, 1995

Whatley, Christopher A., *Bought and Sold for English Gold?* East Linton, 2001

SOURCES

Defoe's Letters: Royal Commission on Historical Manuscripts, Report of the Royal Commission on Historical Manuscripts, London 1870-1899, Report Fifteen, Appendix IV, 1899

Defoe's Review

Defoe's Review, A Facsimile edition by Arthur Wellesley Secord, 9 vols., Columbia, 1938

Defoe's Pamphlets: The vast majority of these are available on microfilm in the series, *The Eighteenth Century*, Woodbridge, 1982. Extracts from the anonymous The Review Review'd. In a Letter to the Prophet Daniel in Scotland, London, 1707 come from Novak, Maximilian, 'A Whiff of Scandal in the Life of Daniel Defoe', *Huntingdon Library Quarterly*, 35-42

Colonel Jack

The Novels and Miscellaneous Works of Daniel De Foe, vol. 1. London, 1854

INDEX